Narrating Demons, Transformative Texts

Narrating Demons, Transformative Texts

Rereading Genius in Mid-Century Modern Fictional Memoir

DANIEL T. O'HARA

THE OHIO STATE UNIVERSITY PRESS • COLUMBUS

Library of Congress Cataloging-in-Publication Data
O'Hara, Daniel T., 1948–
  Narrating demons, transformative texts : rereading genius in mid-century modern fictional memoir / Daniel T. O'Hara.
       p. cm.
  Includes bibliographical references and index.
  ISBN 978-0-8142-1179-3 (cloth : alk. paper)—ISBN 978-0-8142-9280-8 (cd)
       1. Literature, Modern—20th century—History and criticism. 2. Genius in literature. 3. Mann, Thomas, 1875–1955. Doktor Faustus. 4. Nabokov, Vladimir Vladimirovich, 1899–1977. Lolita. 5. Burroughs, William S., 1914–1997. Naked lunch.
  I. Title.
    PN771.O37 2012
    809.392553—dc23
                                    2011036067

Paper (ISBN: 978-0-8142-5670-1)
Cover design by Larry Nozik.
Type set in Adobe Minion Pro.

9 8 7 6 5 4 3 2 1

To Jonathan Arac, Paul Bove, and Donald Pease:

Brothers!

The separable meanings of each word . . . are here brought into one. And as they come together, as the reader's mind finds cross-connection after cross-connection between them, he seems, in becoming more aware of them, to be discovering not only Shakespeare's meaning [in *Venus and Adonis*], but something which he, the reader, is himself making. His understanding of Shakespeare is sanctioned by his own activity in it. As Coleridge says: "You feel him to be a poet, inasmuch as for a time he has made you one—an active creative being."

—I. A. Richards,
Coleridge on the Imagination (1934, 1960)

Brand X

I have always been in love with Brand X.
As a kid I'd see those commercials with
the brand name TV set right beside Brand X:
The crystal clear picture next to the snowy one—
which to me was really more starry—the way
it looks in your head after hitting your elbow.
Who'd ever want to buy a product like that?
Which is partially why I've loved Brand X.

But my father may have expressed the better
reason best : "Brand X lets you tinker with it"—
to repair, to improve—as though endlessly
customizing.

     But Zenith (the best set then)
once it went it went all at once—as with
a model atomic flash—nothing like Brand X:
Trying out both, we made the perverse choice.

Contents

Preface

I BEGAN WORKING on this book project some thirty years ago after noticing how the tropes and techniques intimately associated with modernism—irony, parody, unreliable point of view—while still present and active in certain "big" or important novels of the post-war period no longer determined the way to read them. The three "classics" or canonical novels of this kind, all fictional memoirs—not just as it turns out—are *Doctor Faustus* (1947), *Lolita* (1955), and *Naked Lunch* (1959), the subjects of my readings here. Two of these became iconic for post-war American culture, and the third definitively identified Nazism with the Devil. An old cultural icon resuscitated then, and two newly minted ones. Teaching and researching these novels, transformative of the idea of genius, of culture, of the literary, over this long period finally let me feel comfortable writing about them.

Because I grew up during the time now-dubbed mid-century modern, my first idea, many offshoots of which still remain, was to focus on what the epigraphic poem of mine calls "Brand X culture." Kitsch and classic merge to become all one incredibly vulgar pop culture that we like, perversely enough, because we can play with it and customize it to our liking. Certainly, the "progress" in this direction can be read in my selection of iconic texts, *Naked Lunch* being a collective product if ever there was one.

But there were those nagging questions of point of view, of irony, of parody, of pastiche, of modernism and postmodernism. And then it hit me: these three influential novels, the first a perfected model for how to do the great novel as a fictional memoir, the other two presenting new models of what counts as "normally" human as narrated by the excluded themselves, always sounded in their key moments entirely sincere. This is not to claim that there are no previous examples of such things. *Frankenstein* and *The Confessions of an Opium Eater* come immediately to mind. But the latter, neither in its time nor in ours, became a widespread permanent cultural icon, and the former did so in our time only because of its film adaptations.

The more I thought about my select group of novels, the more I focused on the culture of genius they instantiated and sought to revise. The other side of Brand X culture is the worship of genius, of the Zenith TV set over the Dumont. During the first half of the Cold War, for all the obvious historical reasons, U.S. culture aimed to produce geniuses in all fields. As the Nobel Prizes piled up for America, especially in literature—Buck (1936), O'Neill (1938), Eliot (1948), Faulkner (1950), Hemmingway (1954), Steinbeck (1962)—writers competed to be recognized as a genius even as the idea lost its remaining intellectual substance in Brand X culture. So why, then, did the writers of the time choose to narrate the fictional lives of such characters as a somewhat reluctant Satan worshipper (Adrian Leverkuhn) who deliberately contracts syphilis to force his diseased brain into the state of genius; a psychopathic pedophilic kidnapper (Humbert Humbert), who claims that Lolita is a demonic nymphet and he himself is a hapless genius seduced by her; and a homicidal/suicidal-gay-drug-addict-part-time detective (William Lee)? They did so because the international culture of genius they were hardwired by was turbo-charged—to mix metaphors appropriately—by America (Mann lived in LA while composing *Doctor Faustus*) which celebrated and catered to genius, and they were driven to try to blow up that culture from within by including in their fictional memoirs the very kinds of characters America defined as aberrant and dangerous. Genius itself was aberrant and dangerous, not to mention the tendencies and experiences they themselves may have known all too well. The cost of genius, if it exists, they knew by their rueful pursuit of it, was high.

The theory of the great writer and the masterpiece, of the imaginative genius, that dominated the period is best summarized by Lionel Trilling, as I present it in the introductory first chapter. Essentially, it is that the great writer both in himself and in his masterpiece—yes, it is an all-male affair, I'm afraid—contain a greater portion, a more intense concentrate, of the culture's oppositions and conflicts and represent them as such: the great Yes and the great No, of the writer's historical moment. How the great writer or genius resolves or reconciles these conflicts and oppositions is in an imaginative dialectical synthesis, a kind of *noblesse oblige* on the part of the genius. In his masterpiece, he gives to us a per-fected expression of usually tragic insight into the human condition via his identification with his less-than-adequate modern hero. Joyce is the model for this action, as Trilling sees it, but we certainly can think of many other examples. What better way for Mann, Nabokov, and Bur-roughs to explode this culture of genius from within than to make their eloquently self-destructive "heroes" the criminally insane?

But what about a positive view of genius to replace Trilling's and the culture's? For that, I have turned to Spinoza. Yes, I know: Spinoza? Really? I had read Spinoza first nearly fifty years ago in college, then again during the late 1980s and early 1990s when there was a Spinoza boomlet largely due to Deleuze's influence, and recently in a reading group setting with colleagues and graduate students. I remembered this time around the great book by Thomas McFarland, *Coleridge and the Pantheistic Tradition* (1969), which I read in graduate school. What struck me this time around with Spinoza was how much the *Ethics,* despite its geometrical method and rationalist goals, read like a romantic heterocosm, that would-be textual whole that is really a fragment of the literary system or absolute analyzed so well by Lacouthe-Labarthes and Nancy. It was Spinoza's cos-mology of the literary universe, as it were, except that Spinoza thought it was less a cosmology than an instance of the cosmos and its God at work that the *Ethics* proposes. But to me, a confirmed Nietzschean, every text is a would-be heterocosm, an other-world with its own "god" or genius permeated throughout it and the expression of the highest power-state known to the writer in question. Such being the case, then, every word of that textual world is meant as part of that world, especially as the idea of transcendence fades and that of immanence grows. Horizontal relations of all kinds replace vertical hierarchies with a vengeance, globally. Rather than each text, certainly each masterpiece, composing differences into hierarchical structures of binary oppositions atop which sits the author-figure projected by the text like a vision of the traditional creator-god over his world, we now have, as Spinoza puts apropos his metaphysics their identification, *Deus sive Natura*. All the distinctions existing in previous hierarchies reappear as versions of activity (*Natura naturans*) and passivity (*Natura naturata*) within an ever-spreading field of power, pleasure, and potential blessedness via greater knowledge of the field. However bizarre it may sound, I saw that the last two novels here especially instantiate such a vision, and the first novel, while closing down the last modernist vision of hierarchy, also opens up the new vista. The reason why I only begin putting Spinoza explicitly to work with *Lolita* and *Naked Lunch*, and not with *Doctor Faustus*, lies here. Whether we think of these texts as new stars in the firmament or as new black holes, there they are: to be read as best we can.

Acknowledgments

TO ALAN SINGER for his continued support and critical powers of reading and to the other members of the Spinoza reading group, especially Phillip Mahoney and Michelle Martin, I express my profound gratitude. To my friends and *boundary 2* colleagues to whom this book is dedicated I owe the best that is in me or my work: endless shared imagination.

A different version of the second chapter has appeared in *Soundings* 93, 1–2 (Spring/Summer 2010), 601–24.

CHAPTER I

The Culture of Genius at Mid-Century

Genius is a gift that never appears such, like what it gives.
—Derrida

DERRIDA'S RECENT deconstructive version of genius is so much like his paradoxical theory of the gift (to be a gift it dare not seem to give) that it does not generally help illuminate any specific understanding of genius. His stress on its event character, however, does serve. In its long history, the idea of genius takes on many forms, but all of them testify to the sudden, unexpected manifestation of genius. This is so whether one means by the term the guardian spirit or daemon (*daimon* in Greek) attached to a person at birth and symbolized by one's guiding star in astrology; or if one means a power or ability, a capacity beyond the ordinary identified as one's own and found in what we have produced or done. Sometimes, of course, one's daemon or genius is not good but evil, not a special creation of God or the gods (like guardian angels or *geni loci*) but the soul of an illustrious dead man (usually) bent imperiously on working off his guilt or fulfilling unfulfilled designs via the person with whom the ghost shares a psyche—Hamlet's father's "Remember me" with a vengeance. Whatever the case may be, when genius bursts forth it realizes virtue in the old Renaissance sense, a power of invention and act that is swift and decisive whether in art or politics.[1]

A key to understanding the secular culture of genius at mid-century is to recognize that there is a consensus about what in art, in literature especially, the imagination of the great writer does. Modernist and New Critical adaptations of Coleridge on the imagination and the action of the poet, ideally considered; or dialectical models derived from Marx or Hegel; or Freudian conceptions of creative daydreaming and sublimation—all demonstrate how mid-century intellectuals, particularly in the U.S., conceive of great writers as powerful or "first-rate minds" containing, so as to incorporate in their works, the binary oppositions splitting and conflicting the culture. Lionel Trilling in "Reality in America" (an essay originally in two parts published in 1940 and 1946 and then revised for inclusion in *The Liberal Imagination* in 1950) lays out the consensus view of what the great writer, the genius, accomplishes via his work for a culture.[2]

> A culture is not a flow, nor even a confluence; the form of its existence is struggle, or at least debate—it is nothing if not a dialectic. And in any culture there are likely to be certain artists who contain a large part of the dialectic within themselves, their meaning and power lying in their contradictions; they contain within themselves, it may be said, the very essence of the culture, and the sign of this is that they do not submit to serve the ends of any one ideological group or tendency. It is a significant circumstance of American culture, and one which is susceptible of explanation, that an unusually large proportion of its notable writers in the nineteenth century were such repositories of the dialectic of their times—they contained both the yes and the no of their culture, and by that token they were prophetic of the future. (76)

Whether this containment policy model of genius echoes prophetically what becomes the geo-politics of the U.S. vis-à-vis the Soviet Union after 1947 is an interesting question to explore on another occasion. But what it does mean is that whether at the level of literary texture or structure, or in terms of psycho-biographical reading of the literary work, the great writer or genius internalizes in imaginative terms, pregnant with a future, the conflicts of the cultural moment. One-time fellow traveling social critics, New Critics, and psychoanalytic critics can all agree on this containment of conflict formulation of the culture of genius.

One word missing from Trilling's brilliant formulation, of course, is "resolution." How does—if he does—the great writer resolve or reconcile the conflicting oppositions marking the works of genius? The resolution that Trilling assumes in his readings for most of his representative critical career is not fully articulated until his 1967 commentary on Joyce's "The Dead."[3]

Trilling agrees with commentators who read Gabriel Conroy as a prototype for that particularly modern creature, the person with considerable imagination but little of the power of execution required to produce a work of genius, perhaps not even for mediocre work. Trilling, like Hugh Kenner, reads Joyce as filleting his protagonist with irony after irony, not the least of ironies being the final revelation that his wife, Greta, after whom he now lusts as they are bedding down for the night in a Dublin hotel room, is all the time thinking of young tubercular Michael Furey, her first lover, whom she still believes died for his love of her by standing outside her room and serenading her on a rainy night before she is to go away to convent school, now so many years ago.

The conflict within the international class of modern intellectuals between the admiration and emulation of genius and its imaginative power of achievement is represented for Conroy by this crushing failure of his power to love Greta enough to overcome this ghost of the past. Yet, Trilling goes on to argue, against any finally ironic reading of "The Dead" and more in line with Richard Ellmann's more positive biographical reading, that Joyce, in the last paragraphs of the story, particularly in the last paragraph, grants to Gabriel such a greater power of vision and poetic expression that it can only be a gift of his creator's own genius.[4]

This sudden identification of the author with his character is one of the most striking and effective elements of the story. Joyce feels exactly what Conroy feels about the sadness of human life, its terrible nearness to death, and the *waste* that every life is; he directs no irony upon Conroy's grief, but makes Conroy's suffering his own, with no reservations whatever. At several points in the story he has clearly regarded Conroy's language, or the tone of his thoughts, as banal, or vulgar, or sentimental. But as the story approaches its conclusion, it becomes impossible for us to know whose language we are hearing, Conroy's or the author's, or to know to whose tone of desperate sorrow we are responding. It is as if Joyce, secure in his genius and identity, were saying that under the aspect of the imagination of death and death-in-life there is no difference

between him and the mediocre, sentimental man of whom he has been
writing. (117)

The liberal culture of genius entails for its maintenance that its great
writers take upon themselves, contain within themselves, its strident conflicts, and in their works resolve them imaginatively, for a moment, by
magnanimously granting to that culture's most ironically representative
men—mediocre, sentimental all—some measure of their creative power
of language, as in such visions of the snow being "general all over Ireland," which famously concludes "The Dead."

> Generous tears filled Gabriel's eyes. He had never felt like that himself
> towards any woman, but he knew that such a feeling must be love. The
> tears gathered more thickly in his eyes and in the partial darkness he
> imagined he saw the form of a young man standing under a dripping tree.
> Other forms were near. His soul had approached that region where dwell
> the vast hosts of the dead. He was conscious of, but could not apprehend,
> their wayward and flickering existence. His own identity was fading out
> into a grey impalpable world: the solid world itself, which these dead had
> one time reared and lived in, was dissolving and dwindling.
>
> A few light taps upon the pane made him turn to the window. It had
> begun to snow again. He watched sleepily the flakes, silver and dark, fall-
> ing obliquely against the lamplight. The time had come for him to set out
> on his journey westward. Yes, the newspapers were right: snow was gen-
> eral all over Ireland. It was falling on every part of the dark central plain,
> on the treeless hills, falling softly upon the Bog of Allen and, farther
> westward, softly falling into the dark mutinous Shannon waves. It was
> falling, too, upon every part of the lonely churchyard on the hill where
> Michael Furey lay buried. It lay thickly drifted on the crooked crosses
> and headstones, on the spears of the little gate, on the barren thorns.
> His soul swooned slowly as he heard the snow falling faintly through the
> universe and faintly falling, like the descent of their last end, upon all the
> living and the dead.[5]

Coleridge's vision of the imagination and of the poet's ideal activity are
evoked for the mid-century modern critic by Trilling's reading of this
vision, as is Saint Paul's vision of Jesus reconciling the conflicts of life via
his sacrificial act of salvation. And the demand that the great writer put

his genius to work in just this fashion, incorporating and containing all conflicts—between the ideal and the real, the general and the particular, the universal and the individual, passion and reason, the creative elite and those leading lives of quiet desperation, and so on—means that the genius is also a saint, suffering these conflicts by containing and resolving them as here envisioned.

This vision of the creative imagination working at full tilt always reminds me of the scene in *Rebel without a Cause* (1955) when James Dean, in response to his parents' bickering in the police station over his latest infraction of the law, screams at them, "You are tearing me apart!" Trilling's severe demand, placed upon the would-be great writer or artist, can only lead in the final analysis to forms of crack-up all too familiar to us from post-Romantic literary history generally and American literary history in particular. Whether we think of the long tradition of the *poète maudit* or its more recent "lost generation" or "Jazz Age" versions, or look forward to prime examples from the Beat or Countercultural generations, we see the evident consequences of aspiring to genius within this cultural moment. The best minds of generation after generation are lost to their "madness."

Moreover, when the conflicts that the genius is to represent and imaginatively express in an ideal form of reconciliation or resolution, predictive of the future, are totally intractable, so that the culture itself can fairly be judged to be "mad," it is expected that its supposedly more-than-human, or daemonically imaginative, artists may not just expire in the attempt to write but turn positively daemonic themselves, not only increasingly against the culture but against themselves in their failures to measure up. Loathing of their culture and of themselves becomes the double-bind legacy of this mid-century modern vision of the imaginative genius.

The most important unintended consequence of this consensus vision of magnanimously ironic containments of conflict for the culture of genius is that despite the warnings, perhaps because of them, of such novels as *Doctor Faustus* about the dubious ideal of genius and its mad breakthroughs at all cost, whether on the individual or national level, the bitterly self-loathing would-be geniuses emerging at this time could readily identify with those aspects of themselves that made them, from the established point of view, unfit to be representative of so-called normal society. The supposedly psychopathic pedophile, the gay and apparently homicidal dope-fiend, like the musical genius making a deal with the devil himself, can become the new sublime figures of imaginative power regardless of whether they serve any discernible prophetically representative or creatively expressive cultural purposes or not. Of course, such purposes can always be discovered if the critic works hard enough. *Lolita* and *Naked Lunch* most readily lent themselves to liberal campaigns at the time to expand the range of acceptable representations of sexual matters. My readings of them, however, focus on the theory of the imagination that is not a version of that dominating the period. Nor is it one that I have seen discussed subsequently. What follows is a theory elaborated out of these works and consolidated by my reading of Spinoza.

Why Spinoza? His is the most radical theory of immanence ever. There is no principle of transcendence anywhere in the system of his *Ethics*.[6] Spinoza's conatus provides the key: only that which enhances our powers and capacities to persist in existence is good; all else is evil. Such spontaneous expression is a singular act. It is, I would argue, genius; all else is external determination alien to our natures. Conatus, the striving for existence and its singular persistence in any instance, is perfected in the self-work appropriate to each form of being. Just as every being is the actualization of Nature or God, so too every self-work as a text is the actualization of a singular conatus in its creation of a world.

God is our model here. He is absolutely free as the perfect expression of all his attributes in all their modes in the world or Nature: he is pure act and is not really—only analytically—distinguishable from his power in action. Our intellectual love of God, the highest form of creativity, is our emulation of such freedom in our lives, seeking to express what arises spontaneously from within ourselves and to defend against what would limit us from doing so. This democratic sense of genius as absolute expression available potentially to all replaces the Trilling sense of representative man and his self-sacrificing noblesse oblige.

Spinoza's *Ethics* is an instance of what it enunciates. It isn't a representation but an expression. It is what it performs, an instance of its vision. The immanence of God in Nature so that *Deus sive Natura* is its motto is itself performed by the author's immanence in the text. The self-work is what this book or this world is for the respective agencies that are their acts of expression. The name of author or of God is the name of the state of creation in these cases. It is the fullest, highest, most blessed state of joy or pleasure in power in action.

We can have sensuous knowledge of a text that is impressionistic at

worst, incomplete at best; we can understand its context and composi-
tional elements, which is better; but we intuit the principles of its formation into the whole that it is. Genre and convention, like reference,
remain at the level of imagination and understanding but do not reach
into the region where the existence, the conatus of the self-work, forms
itself and acts.

The self-work is God in miniature, an infinite of a scope different from
that of God or Nature as a whole but still an infinite. We can know it only
finitely, even when we intuit its principle of formation, because we cannot
know or execute all its modes of actualization. If God is the Genius of his
self-work named Nature (or World), then the author is the genius of the
self-work of the text. In fact, the composite neologism "self-world-work"
would best express what is at stake. The self-work is the repeated creation
of the world.

Of course, the history of contemporary criticism and theory since
mid-century is one in which the author is said to die into the text. But
my theory assumes that this recent development has been the case from
the beginning—there never was transcendence, only immanence. The
author is each word in its place in the text. Like God—or Nature—with
infinite attributes and modes, the author is the text and all that it sum-
mons forth.

What this would mean for the ending of "The Dead" is that Trilling
unnecessarily manufactures distinctions. The imaginative power of language extended throughout the body of the text condenses itself into
what is comparatively a visionary focal point to conclude, bringing beautifully together the story's major themes in ever-softening crescendo, like
the perversely sublime conclusion of "A Day in the Life." We can name
this power of expression Joyce or Joyce via Gabriel or the genius of the
text—or simply God:

> *The mind's intellectual love toward God is the love of God wherewith God
> loves himself not insofar as he is infinite, but insofar as he can be explicated
> through the essence of the human mind considered under a form of eternity.
> That is, the mind's intellectual love toward God is part of the infinite love
> wherewith God loves himself.* (157, original italics)

Unlike the Lacanian Big Other of the Symbolic Order, Spinoza's God is
more like that of some schizophrenics, a power of inflowing energies

apparently without cessation. Acts of power. There is no internal screen. Such a God (or Nature) is more like Freud's Id than like Trilling's heroically self-sacrificing, magnanimously noble genius. These two models of sublime imagination define the parameters of mid-century modern culture, whether we think of Jackson Pollock or Leonard Bernstein.

Spinoza in the *Ethics* produces a modern philosophical heterocosm that purports to be a model of the cosmos and God's workings in (and as) it. Spinoza replaces the distinction between God and Nature with their equivalence, *Deus sive Natura*. The geometrical method of argument in the *Ethics* is an instance and demonstration of how the causal necessity works in the universe. The one substance that is *Deus sive Natura* possesses the attributes of both thought and extension in infinite and finite modes, or ways of being. The intellectual love of God is blessedness because it leads to the fullest and highest kind of knowledge and so the greatest mode of power possible for humans. With such knowledge of the laws of Nature and of God (they are of course the same) we can create the conditions that can give us the maximum opportunity to determine our actions solely from internal causes, rather than suffer via our passions from external causes.

There are several major questions debated by commentators: Is Spinoza's position tantamount to pantheism or atheism? What are the specific relationships among the attributes, and possibly other attributes unknowable by us, modes (infinite and finite), and individual beings? Does the immanence of Spinoza's position make for a night in which all cows are black, as Hegel charges, repeating his satire of Schelling against Spinoza? Why is immanence a good thing, transcendence not? My concern is not for any of these questions. The theory of genius, of the creative imagination, which I am advocating sees Spinoza's philosophical system as a template for the kind of heterocosmic imagination that operates in the works of mid-century fictional memoir read here. I will argue in a subsequent book for such a theory as being the best guide to reading the central Romantic and post-Romantic texts from Blake, Wordsworth and Coleridge, Freud and Mann, to the present moment.

What I am claiming and hopefully demonstrating here is that the modern works that achieve canonical status do so because they are new models of literature productive of more literature to come. The analogy would be with new cosmologies, except that to fit my meaning more precisely the latter would have to be new cosmoses too. The closer to being sui generis, the greater the work. What we read as allusion, irony, parody, pastiche, and so on, is part of our horizon of critical understanding, but the works themselves are entirely sincere and univocal in their construction of their models of literature, making use of whatever is lying around the cultural yard. We do best to read such works literally. Of course, the burden of the book to follow is to make good on these admittedly provocative claims.

A few words in conclusion about the selection of works: *Doctor Faustus* captures the late modernist turn as it emerges into a postmodernism we are now very familiar with. The final twist in the novel occurs when the reader realizes that the humanist narrator, Serenus Zeitblum, may be as much of a devil's disciple as Adrian Luverkuhn, the sublime musical genius, and yet Mann is entirely sincere about his vision of a hope beyond hopelessness for Germany, for Europe, and for the modern world as a whole. For the reader treads on new ground different from that of the ironic, self-defeating allegories of modern fiction that repeat in a finer, albeit self-reflexive, tone, the models of literature derived from myth and traditional culture à la *The Waste Land* and *Ulysses*. Although producing no new model of literature, *Doctor Faustus* does close down the old modernist one, and prepares the opening for what is to come.

Both *Lolita* and *Naked Lunch* achieve iconic cultural status generally and are best read in light of what the theory of genius out of Spinoza that I propose can illuminate. Or so it is what the rest of the book would hope to show.

CHAPTER 2

Of Love and Death in Modern Culture

Rereading *Doctor Faustus* with Freud in Mind

For Paul A. Bove

From the depths of dark solitude. From
The eternal abode in my holiness,
Hidden set apart in my stern counsels
Reserv'd for the days of futurity,
I have sought with a joy without pain
For a solid without fluctuation
Why will you die O Eternals?
Why live in unquenchable burnings?
    —William Blake, *The Book of Urizen*, Ch. II, St. 4

THE FIRST TIME I discussed Thomas Mann's 1947 novel *Doctor Faustus: The Life of the German Composer Adrian Leverkuhn As Told by a Friend* was in the early 1980s.[1] The occasion was an annual special session at the Modern Language Convention entitled "Defining Modernism." My memory of the details of panel membership is a bit vaguer than I would like, but I believe that I, along with Paul Bove and Jonathan Arac, *boundary 2* colleagues, were panelists, as was Professor Stanley Corngold, a Germanist and an expert on Mann and Kafka from Princeton. I was interested in *Doctor Faustus* because I wanted to understand why and how irony transforms itself into parody, a general literary phenomenon in the last century, which some more famous critics then were beginning to say marked the defining difference between modernism and postmodernism.[2]

I believed that I could clearly see this revisionary process at work in the novel, in part thanks to R. P. Blackmur's chapter on it in *Eleven Essays in the European Novel*, a text Paul Bove originally suggested to me.[3] Mann referred to this revisionary process under the heading of "erotic irony" in his *Story of a Novel: The Genius of Doctor Faustus*, which is made out of sections from his diary about the composition of the novel. Also the then just-translated 1918 text by Mann, *Reflections of a Non-Political Man*, with an entire chapter devoted to "erotic irony," also supported this view.[4] Mann first deployed this term here in the earlier text *Reflections* and then developed, revised, and put it into masterful play in *Faustus*, commenting on it as well in those selective diary entries compiled and revised afterwards in *Story of a Novel*. This over-determined circling around the topic caught my eye. Specifically, I saw in erotic irony the weight of the powerful drive that transformed a measured self-irony into an infinite-seeming self-parody.[5] In short, I thought I could use "erotic irony" to give a convincing account of why twentieth-century literary culture, as represented so effectively by Mann's mid-century masterpiece, turned ever more relentlessly, self-destructively, even demonically against itself. This was the substance of my talk, entitled "The Self-Destructive Imagination in *Doctor Faustus*."

The arguments of the other session presentations are now a blur, of course, but the question period, at least its beginning, is etched in my mind like an Albrecht Dürer engraving of Death. For after we spoke, the first question came from a surprise guest, Edward W. Said, who given the time-frame must have been at work on *Faustus* for his book of a few years hence, *Musical Elaborations*.[6] In any event, The Worldly Critic Himself now rose to ask what he called "a simple, even a naive question" of us all. "Why, when discussing *Doctor Faustus*, a novel Adorno helps make centrally about Schoenberg's twelve-tone musical system," Said inquired, "did none of you even mention music?" Imagine not a note about contrapuntal glissando from any of us would-be critical emperors of irony, parody, modernism and postmodernism, or whatever, who now stood exposed, before an overflow crowd, for the bunch of naked asses we then rightly appeared to be. Not one of us, I also remember all too well, could offer any satisfactory answer.

Thus, my current discussion is my belated answer to Said, twenty-seven years after the fact. By the way, in case you are wondering, I will discuss music, but only briefly, at the end of the chapter.[7] Even today, I still do not think the novel is really about modern music, despite half of the latest German edition's 741 pages being devoted to it. Instead, it is about loving genius and its tragic cost.[8]

With that, since this novel may not be that familiar, I provide the description of *Doctor Faustus* on the back of the latest English translation.

> Thomas Mann's last great novel, first published in 1947 and now newly rendered into English by acclaimed translator John E. Woods, is a modern reworking of the Faust legend, in which Germany sells its soul to the Devil. Mann's protagonist, the composer Adrian Leverkuhn, is the flower of German culture, a brilliant, isolated, overreaching figure, his radical new music a breakneck game played by art at the very edge of impossibility. In return, for twenty-four years of unparalleled musical accomplishment, he bargains away his soul—and the ability to love his fellow man. Leverkuhn's life story is a brilliant allegory of the rise of the Third Reich, of Germany's renunciation of its own humanity and its embrace of ambition and nihilism. It is also Mann's most profound meditation on the German genius—both national and individual—and the terrible responsibilities of the truly great artist.

What a simple story—and so sensational—in its old-fashioned way! But somewhat inaccurate. Like many commentators, even Said in *Musical Elaborations,* there is no mention of how the story is told—"As Told by a Friend." And as told by Serenus Zeitblom (Serene Time-Bloom or Time-Bloom, as I prefer), the philologist and self-described pedagogue, the parallels between the rise of the Third Reich and the career of Leverkuhn remain just that, parallels with important differences between them.

First of all, Zeitblom fears throughout the novel that his friend's works, condemned by the Nazis, will never see the light of day no matter which side wins World War II. This is the period during most of which the novel is fictionally and actually composed. Wagner is more their speed than Leverkuhn, and Cole Porter more the Allies' cup of tea. Second, we never see Germany make a bargain with the Devil, not even "symbolically" by accepting Hitler. What we do see, through his own words in a letter, is Adrian make such a deal. Leverkuhn's productive life ends with his madness, in 1930, three years before Hitler and his goons take over Germany. I do agree that ambition and nihilism play their roles, but even more so does the tangled web of love and genius. Lastly, however, just to mention the big point this blurb gets wrong, *Doctor Faustus* is not an allegory, brilliant or otherwise; it is a strangely inverted tragic novel, the last of the modernist novels and the first of the postmodernist kind. I will explain why I say this shortly, but first my necessary explanation of "erotic irony."

Unlike *Reflections of a Non-Political Man* and *Doctor Faustus, Death in Venice* (1911) never uses the words "erotic irony," but it presents it at work beautifully.[9] Gustave Aschenbach, on holiday in Venice, falls in love with a fourteen-year-old Polish boy Tadzio for his incredible beauty. This beauty is the mirroring bodily image, Aschenbach feels, of the spirit and force, the ideal of beauty, that drive his aspiration to genius and its creation in words. What nature has accidentally done, Aschenbach would do at his own beck and call. The problem is that shortly after being made officially "von Aschenbach" and so a noble on his fiftieth birthday, he has hit a deep and protracted dry spell. This transgressive, even mad love for the boy, however, inspires the accomplished and esteemed middle-aged writer to raptures unknown before. Aschenbach even produces a paean to beauty a page and a half long! In it he recalls Socrates and Phaedrus, describing how the older, ugly philosopher woos the beautiful youth to his philosophy of the eternal forms ("Strangely fruitful intercourse, between one body and another mind!" [414]), Ashenbach concludes his prose-poem. In its middle, he perfectly describes what Mann means by "erotic irony."

> Thought that can merge wholly into feeling, feeling that can merge wholly into thought—these are the artist's highest joy. And our solitary felt in himself at this moment power to command and wield a thought that thrilled with emotion, an emotion as precise and concentrated as thought: namely, that nature herself shivers with ecstasy when the mind bows down in homage before beauty. (413)

Of course, as with youths like Alcibiades, who want more of Socrates than inspired imaginations (an ironic reversal, after all, on the usual way such love works), or like Heloise and Abelard who both end up wanting more than pedagogical routine and have to settle in the end for much less, Aschenbach ends up badly. He ends up stalking Tadzio, staying on much too long in a cholera-plagued Venice to do so, hoping against hope for a general breakdown of order so that the looks and smiles he and Tadzio belatedly share could become something more. Made-up like a much younger man and so looking as clownish as his lust, Aschenbach dies staring out to sea where Tadzio is standing on a shrinking sandbar mysteriously pointing farther out.

Erotic irony is, then, the sacrifice the lover makes in homage to the beloved as the inspiring medium for eternal beauty's actualization that the lover's mind would create in its work, in this case, in literary art. In the mirror of physical beauty the artist sees the image of his creative ideal ready to be released into existence as a unified and unifying imagination living in and as the work of art, in which thought and feeling, mind and body, are organically one—a classic modernist aesthetic formulation already in 1911! The awful, even terrible cost of such erotic irony, for all concerned, is usually not dwelt upon.

My thesis about *Doctor Faustus* is that it is a novel in which its narrator plays the lover, and its subject, the musical genius Leverkuhn, plays the beloved. This is especially so now that he is dead, with the latter's strangely beautiful avant-garde music, like a Dionysian nature or fracturing world-system, bearing sublime witness to the narrator's acts of loving genius begun during Leverkuhn's life and now completed in composing this fictional life.[10] What many have identified as the Tonio Kroeger effect, the love of the more intelligent and imaginative man for the banal and normal beloved thus suffers a significant variation, an ironic inversion, with the self-declared ordinary and normal man, Zeitblom, bitterly captivated with the alleged musical genius Leverkuhn, who as a person appears to be virtually inhuman. Usually nowadays, of course, we think of this erotic pattern as "smart women, stupid choices."

It is here that for further clarification I must turn to Freud, to Mann's Freud anyway, as Mann celebrates him in his 1936 speech in Vienna on the occasion of his eightieth birthday.[11] With the old man sitting there, Mann concludes "Freud and the Future" with this incredible prophecy, made especially so now given how far Freud's reputation (and humanism's) has fallen in our own times:

[W]e shall one day recognize in Freud's life-work the cornerstone for the building of a new anthropology and therewith of a new structure, to which many stones are being brought today, which shall be the future dwelling of a wiser and freer humanity. This . . . psychologist will . . . be honored as the path-finder towards a humanism of the future, which we dimly divine and which will have experienced much that the earlier humanism knew not of. It will be a humanism standing in a different relation to the powers of the lower world, the unconscious, the id: a relation bolder, freer, blither, productive of a riper art than any possible in our neurotic, fear-ridden, hate-ridden world. . . . Call this, if you choose, a poet's utopia; but the thought is after all not unthinkable that the resolution of our great fear and our great hate, their conversion into a different relation to the unconscious which shall be more the artist's, more ironic and yet not necessarily irreverent, may one day be due to the healing effect of [psychoanalysis]. (426)

Well, even if we only look at the next few years, we have to wonder how wrong a prophecy can be!

What Mann thinks is Freud's key discovery is what he calls "Infantilism" (424), by which he means how the ego, from childhood on, identifies with established roles of family, class, profession, nation, or culture, and so, in this way only, the modern ego is like the ego of antiquity—"open behind" (424) to the past, to the primordial, the legendary, the fabulous, the mythic, in the life of a people or one's own life, which gets repeated forward into the present and future, usually unwittingly for us, but in the case of the great heroes and heroines of the past, quite wittingly. Just as the child plays the game of imitating mommy or daddy, so too the adult would imitate the great figures of the cultural past. Mann's examples are primarily ones such as Cleopatra, Caesar, and other classical figures; but he also claims that this identification is possible anytime, and mentions his own conscious following in Goethe's footsteps. Presumably, he would see this *imitatio dei* pattern at work even with Freud, who after all was ecstatic at winning the 1930 Goethe Prize for Literature. Clearly, too, in *Faustus* Mann is also following in the footsteps of Nietzsche, the would-be music-loving and -creating philologist-philosopher. By the way, one way of understanding Mann's comment in *Story of a Novel* (54) that Zeitblom and Luverkuhn possess the same identity, beyond the obvious case of their being the author's characters, is that they split the Nietzschean paradigm in two. The cultural formulas of two Goethean souls in one breast, the Hegelian unhappy consciousness, are here given a Dionysian boost.

The poet's new humanistic utopia that Mann envisions as being a consequence of the triumph of Freud's therapeutic vision is one in which anyone can wittingly participate in this reanimation of myth and be like Christ on the cross, who at his crisis hour cries out "*Eli, Eli, lama sabachthami*"—not as an act of final despair but as a climactic confirmation of living "life . . . as quotation" (425), since, as Mann glosses Christ's outcry, "Jesus was [not expressing] despair and disillusionment; but on the contrary a lofty messianic sense of self, for Jesus is quoting from the prophecies of the messiah and so the quotation really meant: 'Yes, it is I!' Precisely thus did Cleopatra quote when she took the asp to her breast to die; and again the quotation meant: 'Yes, it is I'" (425). A poet's utopia indeed! Or at least a decadent modern aesthete's, a life of allegory beyond even Keats's imagining?

Freud must have been taken aback by Mann's lecture celebrating his achievement, his life-work, in this way. While Mann mentions some of Freud's works with praise, especially, not surprisingly, *Totem and Taboo*, his characterization of Freud's future legacy sounds less like what Mann calls "the science of the unconscious" (428) and more like what Jung claimed to have discovered, the virtually occult collective unconscious, that global archive of mythic archetypes, and the ways human beings identify with its figures, consciously or not. It is Jung, of course, a Nazi sympathizer, for whom the unconscious in this sense encourages what Paul Bove sees as the disastrous tangle of utopianism, messianism, and visionary allegory all of a humanistic bent.[12]

There is much in "Freud and the Future" that deserves critical analysis, but that is for another occasion. What I want to stress here is that Mann concludes his lecture by assimilating the Jewish Freud to the German romantic tradition via the figure of Faust:

> Freud once called his theory of dreams "a bit of scientific new-found land won from superstition and mysticism." The word "won" expresses [the colonizing spirit of the scientific pioneer] and [the] spirit of his work. "Where id was, shall be ego," he epigrammatically says. And he calls analysis a cultural labour comparable to the draining of the Zuider Zee. Almost in the end the traits of the venerable man merge into the lineaments of the grey-haired Faust, whose
>
> Spirit urges him

To shut the imperious sea from the shore away,
Set narrower bounds to the broad water's waste.

Then open I to many millions space
Where they may life, not-safe-secure, but free
And active. And such a busy swarming I would see
Standing amid free folk on a free soil.
The free folk [Mann concludes] are the people of a future freed from fear
and hate, and ripe for peace. (428)

The topical echoes in 1936 of the infamous Nazi demands for *Lebensraum* (living-space) mingle uncomfortably with what is already an uncomfortable performance. Not only does Mann assimilate Freud to the German romantic tradition, in which science is in the service of the folk and associates easily with occult and even demonic phantasmagoria; he also identifies Freud and his discovery, psychoanalysis, as part and parcel of the Western colonialist adventure. Of course, it is all for the good, as rather sentimentally, utopianly, humanistically envisioned here. And Freud certainly famously declared himself to be more a conquistador than a scientist, a judgment we mostly share now; and too in *Moses and Monotheism*, which appears three years later, what Freud himself referred to as his scientific "novel," he practices an equally strange and paradoxical form of cultural revisionism. Freud would "prove" that Moses, founder of the Jewish people as we still know them, really had to be an Egyptian. Just so as not to overlook any obvious echoes in the concluding passage cited above, the quotation from Freud that Mann cites about the theory of dreams being a scientific "new found land" cannot help making those familiar with the English literary tradition think of John Donne's "The Canonization," which uses the analogy of the discovery of America as the lover's celebratory exclamation made in excited response to the sudden revelation of the beloved's exquisite beauty. Since Mann read and reread Shakespeare and the other English Renaissance poets during the composition of his *Faustus,* it is no wonder there is this echo, too.

In light of erotic irony in this elaborated sense, what, then, is all that music doing in *Doctor Faustus*? I think it is best seen as the creative imagination of Adrian Leverkuhn's beloved genius by the narrator, Serenus Zeitblom, who loves him that much. Its greatness, expressed in the finest detail of contemporary critical theory, is the philologist's work, his gift, however ambiguous and ambivalent it at times appears. We all recall, I think, what Freud said about gifts! Given the obscurity of Leverkuhn's music, the opposition of the Nazi regime to it, the radically uncertain future it faces, not to mention its studied animus to all things popular or easy to take—all of which the narrator notes repeatedly as World War II reaches its climactically destructive end—we must remember that the only testimony to its genius we ever hear is Zeitblom's lovesick praise. Seeing the music in the novel in this way is why I did not think it necessary to mention it way back when. It just seemed so obviously so. I only wish that twenty-five years ago, on that MLA panel, I had not been made tongue-tied by Said's initial critical intervention.

In saying this, I do not intend to dismiss the incredible detail of the musical theories, or the historical discussions of music and its major figures, or the powerfully imaginative if often impressionistic responses of the narrator to his hero's masterpieces. As any lover knows, and my earlier discussion of "Death in Venice" confirms, it is the highly crafted details of the gift of our love that trace the lineaments of our desire. And for purposes of looking at the role of such visions of music that the narrator ascribes to his hero, we do not need to become even amateur experts in the subject. We can simply recall many examples from the history of the novel of similar expressions, from *Don Quixote* on; or at the entire starry panoply of cosmic order in *The Divine Comedy*. All, all are the blazons of love.

Serenus Zeitblom's love for Adrian Leverkuhn is not an entirely happy love, to say the least. Adrian possesses that kind of genius easily bored. As a beginning student, once shown the basics, he can then foresee all the possible elaborations of a subject. That is, once he knows the principles, he grows bored with the details of getting the results. They are for others to learn from. A top student nevertheless, Adrian is not popular with his teachers. He is not a good student in their eyes, precisely because he does not work things out unless he is forced to do so. Given his anticipatory intellectual superiority, he is also highly disdainful, with a laugh that cuts other people down to size, making them self-conscious of their own comparative smallness. Moreover, Adrian apparently cannot recall their names despite long familiarity. Long before the deal with the Devil, who makes him swear off any feelings of love, Serenus at the end of the first chapter admits apropos of Adrian, "All around him lay coldness," a dreadful and demonically prophetic coldness. But the narrator goes even further in his disappointed, unrequited lover's admission, an admission he repeats pretty much in these terms throughout the novel: "I might compare his [self-imposed] isolation [amidst others] to an abyss into which the feelings others expressed for him vanished soundlessly without a trace" (8). And with growing bitter vehemence, as our narrator tells his story he openly includes himself in the camp of the others.

Of course, Serenus is no genius. A philologist who teaches classical languages and culture in the high school, with occasional sojourns as a part-timer in a local college, Zeitblom describes himself as a Catholic humanist, old-fashioned, bourgeois, happily and long married, who is writing now at the end of the Second World War in early retirement due to his quiet but firm disagreements with the Nazi regime. His sons are in active service to their nation, his wife dutifully cares for him, and his hand trembles as much for his self-consciously ironic—or is it self-parodic—suspicion of his incapacity—intellectual, emotional, rhetorical—as for every remembered crisis and catastrophe of the life he is telling or the increasing reports of bombs falling nearby and major German cities in flames. This montage technique, in which the time of the narrator and the time of the story, along with the time of the future reader, who is addressed as such repeatedly, join in *Doctor Faustus* with the modernists' appropriation of Wagner's musical technique of the motif for the text's structure of symbols and images. In doing so, Mann produces some remarkable temporal parallels between the individual life and the historical moment.

Here is how Serenus memorably characterizes himself and his project:

His was an artist's life; and because it was granted to me, an ordinary man, to view it from so close-up, all the feelings of my soul for human life and fate have coalesced around this exceptional form of human existence. For me, thanks to my friendship with Adrian , the artist's life functions as the paradigm for how fate shapes all our lives, as the classic example of how we are deeply moved by what we call becoming, development, destiny—and it probably is so in reality, too. For although his whole life long the artist may remain nearer, if not to say, more faithful to his childhood than the man of practical reality, although one can say that, unlike the latter, he abides in the dreamlike, purely human, and playful state of the child, nevertheless the artist's journey from those pristine early years to the late, unforeseen stages of his development is endlessly longer, wilder, stranger—and more disturbing for those who watch—than that of the everyday person, for whom the thought he, too, was once a child is cause for not half so many tears. (27–28)

As this passage unfolds, though it is never used, I keep hearing the word for culture, *Bildung,* chiming silently. When I check the passage in German, I find that it is not used. Clearly, though, it is insistently suggested by the use of its variants: "*Werden, Entwicklung . . . Schicksals-Gestaltung*" (42): "Becoming, Development, Shape of Destiny or Fateful Design." This method of suggestive allusive implication is how the novel works as much as it does via the techniques of montage and leitmotif. The heard music of the narration is intended to inspire the unheard music in our minds.

Beyond this, the passage reminds us of Goethe and *Dichtung and Wahrheit,* the quintessential romantic statement of the artist's life, which has inspired so many works of autobiography and biography, literal and fictional. The idea of development, *Entwicklung,* is the hallmark of how creative genius gets treated. It is also the way, since Hegel, that first elite and then popular histories of science, philosophy, art, and culture are done. More than this, however, it is also how living organisms have been distinguished from the inorganic realm. And this post-Enlightenment idea of progressive, even dialectical development (despite detours) is also what post-structuralism and deconstruction, following Nietzsche's example, sought to blow up.

And there are many good reasons to do so. Development assumes as its paradigm the individual and generalizes from it to larger units; even in the case of evolution, the focus, until recently, has been on the radiant example, the singular mutation, not the statistical whole. Development, in the case of genius, also entails the sacrifice of others, willing or not, to promote its growth, especially from youth to maturity. As we will see later in the novel, this is a moment when to inspire and facilitate what Zeitblom calls "the breakthrough" into full strength, much is permitted, even encouraged, by way of what used to be called sin but now is more likely to be called transgression. And this idea of development on the macrolevel also has precluded paying close critical attention to how power actually works—using the myth of necessary development to rationalize its usurpation of the state, the party, whatever, with the slaughter, sometimes of millions, as the all-too-usual price that just had to be paid. Finally, in this passage, the narrator would appear to be explicitly making the connection between his life of Luverkuhn and that of Germany. This connection, in its geo-political, even world-historical, dimensions, as well as in others—musical, artistic, sexual—is discussed at length in Chapter XXX, about which much shortly. But right now, I want to look at the cautionary tale the reader receives early on, in Chapter III. Not only should this chapter make us question (but not definitively determine) the narrator's reliability—we have received lots of potential warnings about it, beginning on page 1, most of them coming from the narrator himself; it should also make us question any attempt to make connections in which one side of an opposition would subsume the other in a higher, dialectical synthesis. For such attempts are shown to be matters of myth and faith, of deceptive and self-deceptive illusion—aesthetic play too readily taken for truth. If I am reading *Doctor Faustus* right, it would repeal all of that Western tradition of loving genius without presenting all its tragic consequences.

The third chapter of *Doctor Faustus* is where we hear about Adrian's first contact with the odd combination of modern science and the occult, specifically necromancy, which, as Serenus tells it, haunts his life. Adrian's father, Jonathan, a good wholesome German farmer (Zeitblom's father, by the way, is a pharmacist in the local town) loves to "speculate the elements" (16). That is, he loves to conduct experiments that demonstrate, by tempting Nature to reveal her secrets, how the distinction between the truly living and the demonically animated dead blurs into shining in-distinction via such a compounding of ambiguities, ironies, and paradoxes. The sheer weight of phenomena forces one to give up all such binary oppositions in uneasy despair (the narrator's response), in rueful faith (Father Leverkuhn's response), or madly sounding knowing laughter (Adrian's response), rather than resulting in any happy Hegelian synthesis.

The chapter details ten experiments that Jonathan Leverkuhn loves to perform for the enlightenment and entertainment of himself and his family, especially the boys Adrian and Serenus. They involve demonstrations of protective mimicry (moths, butterflies, leaves) in which one organism will ape the appearance of another, down to its flaws, so as to be also judged unpalatable or poisonous by enemies, to blend in with its surroundings, and so on. But also there are experiments with Chaldini's sand figures, in which the scraping of a violin bow at the end of the metal disk on which sand is cast will cause the sand to assume the wave figures of the notes played. There are also observations of shells from the deepest oceans with what appear to be hieroglyphic inscriptions on them, but for what purpose? They live in nearly total darkness and have no chance of being "read" in any way imaginable. There are also experiments with ice and other types of crystals that mimic uncannily all the features of living organisms and create whole miniature living-looking cities from the floors of their tanks, as with a tap of a magic wand at the sides. Serenus's long comment on these things is worth quoting in full:

> Were these [inorganic] phantasmagoria an imitation of plant life, or were they the pattern of it?—that was [Jonathan's] question. Neither, he presumably replied to himself; they were parallel formations. Nature in her creative dreaming, dreamt the same thing both here and there, and if one spoke of imitation, then certainly it had to be reciprocal. Should one take the children of the soil as models because they possessed the depth of organic reality, whereas the ice flowers were merely external phenomena? But as phenomena, they were the result of an interplay of matter no less complex than that found in plants. If I understood our friendly host correctly, what concerned him was the unity of animate and so-called inanimate nature, the idea that we sin against the latter if the boundary we draw between the two spheres is too rigid, when in reality it is porous, since there is no elementary capability that is reserved exclusively for living creatures or that the biologist could not likewise study on inanimate models. (21)

I take seriously this idea of "parallel formations"—which in the German text are "*Parallelbildungen*" (33). In this composite formulation *bildung* appears, which does mean formation, but also, as we know, "culture," the word I heard in a previous passage as if it were anticipating this one. The evocative albeit equivocal irony of this coinage in *Faustus* stands as fair warning over an interpreter's reading. Nonetheless, I will take the plunge.

This passage presents a different way of seeing the world and how it has been built up. We see here for what they are the apparently mirror images, which do not solicit, even as they too often have nevertheless inspired, humanity's repeated attempts to mistakenly make connections, usually by subsuming one set of images to another as if their models. At every level of the novel—that of theme, point of view, plot, technique, structure—*Doctor Faustus* should be seen as one of Father Leverkuhn's experiments for demonstrating parallel formations in this sense and in this way of warning. That is, it should be seen in the spirit of an irony about what is being presented that transcends parody and self-parody; or, if you will, a parody to end all parody, an irony to transcend irony, an absolute parody and irony, which turns into a modern form of tragic wisdom. It puts into play the artist's life, politics, philosophy, even music—its theories, history, major figures, and modern developments—so as to present parallel formations, repeating the cautionary lesson of this chapter, over and over again, which the critical reader will carefully observe and respect without resolving the parallelisms into a total order in which one formation or set of formations trumps the others. Is this deconstruction *avant le lettre*? Perhaps, but it is also related to what Adorno's dissertation taught Mann about Kierkegaard, as *The Story of a Novel* says (76).

The major example of not heeding such wisdom born of what I will call, for simplicity's sake, absolute irony is also presented in this chapter via the experiment of "the devouring drop," which can stand as an emblem of the radical and total assimilation of one formation by another:

> And just how confusing the interaction is between the two realms we learned from the "devouring drop," to which more than once Father Leverkuhn fed a meal before our very eyes. A drop of whatever it was— paraffin, or some volatile oil, I don't recall specifically, though I believe it was chloroform—a drop, I say, is not an animal, not even a primitive one, not even an amoeba; one does not assume that it has an appetite, seeks nourishment, knows to retain what is digestible and refuse what is not. But that is precisely what our drop did. It was swimming by itself in a glass of water into which Jonathan had introduced it, probably with a pipette. And what he now did was this: With a pair of pincers he picked up a tiny glass rod, actually a thread of glass coated with shellac, and placed it in the vicinity of the drop. That was all that he did, the drop did the rest. It formed a little convexity on its surface, a sort of mount of conception, through which it then ingested the rod lengthwise. Meanwhile it extended itself, took on a pear shape so as to encompass its prey entirely and not leave either end sticking out; and as it gradually reassumed its spherical shape, more ovoid at first, it began, I give you my word, to dine on the shellac that coated the glass rod and to distribute it throughout its own body. When it had finished and had resumed its globular form, it pushed the utensil, now neatly licked clean, back across to the periphery and out into the surrounding water. (22)

If we take the bait here by reading "the devouring drop" as the essence of being, inorganic and organic, and so beyond good and evil, thereby justifying every transgression by genius, group, nation, or humanity as a whole (vis-à-vis nature), we will have performed the simulacrum of appetite (in all senses) that this passage serves up to us for our critical illumination. Mann in *Doctor Faustus* presents the temptation of modernist aesthetic totality even as he both warns against it and creates a radically equivocal polysemous text that, despite its apparently bumbling narrator's best belated efforts suffers in the end neither premature closure, nor any other kind. *Doctor Faustus* is the transgressive gift of tragic love, in an unreserved imaginative economy, to end all resolving harmonies. This modern wisdom text keeps on giving because, like great love (or absolute irony), it is too difficult to tell from despair.

Paul Bove has definitively shown in his "Misprisions of Utopia: Messianism, Apocalypse, and Allegory" that critical interpretation, as its origins in biblical hermeneutics would suggest, would turn the textual materials of any and every historical moment into a self-congratulatory apocalyptic allegory in which a messiah figure brings ultimate redemption but at the price of universal catastrophe. As we see here with "the devouring drop" scene and will see even more so at the novel's conclusion, the narrator, a philologist after all, finds the temptation to fall into this traditional pattern all but irresistible. Fortunately, by Mann's deft handling of reflexive irony, *Doctor Faustus* contains much material for allegorizing and at least one grand allegory, of course, the pact with the devil, but presents it and any other possible allegory critically as a temptation to be overcome.[13]

Chapter XXX of *Doctor Fausus,* about two-thirds of the way into the novel, is where Serenus Zeitblom attempts to make the connections between Adrian's artist's life and the demonically sexual nature of genius, the modern history of Germany, and the tragic idea of the necessarily transgressive form of development, what the narrator calls "the fatal gift of genius" (318), of every type. The word that he chooses is a good one in German: "the breakthrough." Here is the word and its basic meanings, in itself and as it participates in common idioms, the details of which I omit for convenience's sake: "*Durchbruchs:* falling through (*no art*); emerging appearance; coming through; breaking through; revelation; bursting, perforation; to assert *or* show itself; [Natur] to reveal itself; breakthrough, break open; breach; opening; rise, resurgence."[14] I think this word just about covers it all.

The narrator in Chapter XXX opens with the start of World War I and the general thrilling sense of terrible elation that runs through the German population. He continues by justifying this feeling with the idea that to achieve world-historical status as a nation, a distinctive people must manage a breakthrough into strength and identity, however tragic the cost, even the cost of war. It is so necessary or at least thought to be so necessary (317). Assuming a role on the world stage, the breakthrough is crucial for development; he argues similarly for the modern phase of German art and music. The term used throughout, virtually obsessively, is "the breakthrough." In fact, the term is used so many times that it becomes impossible to count its occurrences.

The phrase that is meant to unite all these senses of "the breakthrough" is translated in the latest English version as "the psychology of the new breakthrough" (323). The German original says only "die Psychologie des *Durchbruchs*" (447), italicizing the word "breakthrough" for emphasis. The original English translation, by the way, is here more faithful to the German than it usually is.[15] So crucial is "the breakthrough" for the narrator, who we must remember is a philologist by training and temperament and so invested in the careful scrutiny and use of words, that when Adrian objects to being concerned with the position of German music in the world, one way or the other, Zeitblom gets angry, for as he sees it, Adrian's work, which is largely still to come, could only be intended for a cosmopolitan audience, indeed for a sophisticated and highly diverse audience, and not for a narrow elite of some provincial would-be avant-garde, such as the intellectuals around him now and throughout the 1920s. Here is how Serenus put an end to this argument:

[A]esthetics is all things, whether their effect is engaging or off-putting, just as . . . the 'grace' has the broadest possible meaning. Aesthetic deliverance or confinement, that is destiny, that is what determines one's happiness or unhappiness, whether one is comfortably at home on this earth or lives in hopeless, if proud isolation. And one need not be a philologist to know that what is ugly is despised. The longing to breakthrough, to break free from confines, being sealed inside what is ugly—you may go right ahead and tell me I am threshing straw, but I feel, have always felt, and will plead again against all crude appearances that this is German *kat exochen,* deeply German, the very definition of Germanness, a psychological state threatened by the poison of loneliness, by eccen-

tricity, provincial standoffishness, neurotic involution, unspoken Satanism. . . . (326)

"I broke off" (326) Zeitblom now says, clearly aware that he has crossed
the line. As we already know from Chapter XXV, he has received the
letter from Adrian in the antique dialectic telling of his bargain with
the Devil. To ensure his breakthrough into twenty-four years of sheer
musical genius, he has agreed to surrender his soul at death and never
to love another during life. However, if he should do so, they will die as
do the two people whom he appears finally to love. Now, with this star-
tling "unspoken Satanism" *faux pas,* Adrian looks at Zeitblom, the color
draining from his face, with a look and then a smile, which are truly
terrible: "The look he directed at me was the look, that familiar look that
made me unhappy—and it mattered little whether it was aimed at me
or someone else—mute, veiled, so coldly aloof as to be almost offensive,
and it was followed by the smile, with lips closed, nostrils twitching in
scorn, and by his turning away" (326). Zeitblom is crushed then and
still as he narrates the incident, speculating that his getting sick at the
front so soon after arrival there was his unconscious way of getting back
to Adrian, who is himself too sick with migraines to fight or give any
service to genius.

What Zeitblom would do via the word "breakthrough" (and the similar "switch-words" as Freud calls them in the dream-work) is to connect
all the dimensions of individual and cultural history in the novel into a
single, coherent whole readable in terms of the aesthetics of recognition
and fame, which in our time has become a matter of a rather cheapened
celebrity. While his narrative differs in important ways from the back-
cover blurb quoted earlier, for example, in its insistence that Adrian's
work does not represent the Nazi regime and its aims, it does overlook
the childhood lesson of parallel formations. *Doctor Faustus* performs this
lesson repeatedly even as its self-confessed bumbling narrator apparently
forgets it. The novel thus holds open all the lines of apparent development
(and their ironic reversals) that its narrator (but not its author) would
connect up and close off so as to form into a total work or masterpiece,
even as he confesses his incompetence at writing. This is more than the
modesty topos. It is the power of the romantic conventions governing
the composition of the modern artist's life. In this ironic manner, *Doctor
Faustus* is a modernist novel, harkening strongly back to romantic tradi-
tions, in the process of becoming a postmodernist one.

The novel's conclusion confirms this view. Leverkuhn creates his last great work, *The Lamentation of Dr. Faustus,* a tragic oratorio, as a revocation of Beethoven's "Ode to Joy" in his Ninth Symphony. Inspired by the terrible death from spinal meningitis of his beloved nephew Nepo (nicknamed Echo), this work takes on the significance of entailing the revocation of the bourgeois epoch from its inception in the Renaissance to the present of the novel, when soon after its composition in 1930, Adrian, in confessing his sins to his friends and family before a private performance, goes hideously mad right before their eyes. "Revocation" in German, by the way, is in its verbal form *zurückziehen:* "to pull *or* draw back; *or* draw away; to withdraw, to retire." It is closely associated, in common idioms, with the notorious Hegelian term for dialectical synthesis, *aufheben,* but principally in the sense of "repeal," not resolution.

The idea of revocation cannot help inspiring in this student of English literature the memory of a famous instance from romantic poetry in which the hero of a minor epic must revoke the curse he pronounced upon his nemesis. In *Prometheus Unbound,* the title figure revokes his condemnation of Jupiter, despite long suffering and the likelihood that repression will return at some future moment once he liberates himself. This renunciation, this revocation, this literal calling back of his curse releases Prometheus, but it is supplemented with a warning that his hope of great things for all may be ruined once more by Jupiter breaking out of his earthly abyss. At that point, Prometheus is to construct out of the ruins of hope a hope beyond hopelessness—a formulation we shall shortly see reappear when we discuss the very end of *Doctor Faustus.* Of course, the trope of the revocation itself can be traced to other sources than Shelley. Mann's immediate source, as his *Story of a Novel* also reports, is Adorno's thesis on Kierkegaard (76).

If the novel ended here, it would be a late great example of apocalyptic modernism, a gesture declaring a plague on everyone's house, including especially one's own. Joyce's "The Dead" memorably ends this way, after holding out half a hope that its male protagonist can be transformed by his pity for his wife suffering from the memory of the young man who appears to have died for her. Yeats's poem "The Second Coming" and *The Tower* volume are chock-full of apparently nihilistic visions. Such ironically apocalyptic modernism haunts even works, like *The Waste Land, Women in Love, A Passage to India,* or *To the Lighthouse,* that end in ironic ambiguity, something that many of Mann's commentators see happening in the case of *Doctor Faustus.*[16] We shall see.

Before heading for the finish line, however, and finally discussing music and so satisfying Said's ghost, I want to sum up where we are so far. My argument is that Mann subtly reverses his usual pattern of erotic irony. Rather than creating a situation where the decadent representative of "the mind bows down in homage before beauty" with the latter being represented by the non-intellectual, Mann has the erotic irony operate between two intellectuals, both from the provinces, who achieve professional success, one of whom is said to be a genius, the other of whom, his lifelong friend, is a self-described "ordinary" man and tells the life of his artist-friend as a complex act of homage and a gift of love. Just as the ecstatic frisson in the usual case results from the sacrifice of intellectual pride and stature to a beautiful figure of otherwise less worth, so here, whatever his limitations and possible sins, Serenus sacrifices himself to Adrian, whose genius is suspect and whose humanity is seriously compromised even before his demonic bargain. One of the real-life parallel formations for this variation on Mann's erotic irony is clearly that of decadent love. Lionel Johnson and Oscar Wilde, as heterosexual and homosexual late-nineteenth-century exemplars, both chose beloveds well below their intellectual and imagination standings. But Mann, as we know now from his *Diaries*, chose similarly, with younger men, although how far any relationship got remains a subject of dispute.[17]

In *Doctor Faustus* Adrian turns to Rudoph Schwerdtfeger, a bisexual friend for whom he composes a violin piece, who betrays him in the end, and whom Adrian, it appears, has deliberately led into a fatal relationship. Adrian in his final madness confesses to doing so, and Serenus all along has believed this to be so. There are, of course, class, pedagogical, and psychological dimensions to erotic irony. The pattern of the older, well-established mentor and the new, young protégé, which goes back to the Greeks, shines through here. Various motivations for this pattern have been given, especially in psychoanalysis—neurotic guilt, self-loathing, narcissism, sadomasochism, and so on. I prefer to note its operative force in the novel rather than speculate on its motive. For all the drama of the novel is focused here, on this relationship, with that of Adrian's representative artist's life and Germany's fateful destiny under the Nazis as background, albeit momentous background. Like an opera to end all operas?

And so we conclude with music after all. I quote fully the relevant passage:

My poor great friend! And when perusing this [last] work from his musical remains, from his own downfall, which prophetically anticipates the downfall and ruin of so much else, how often have I thought of the painful words he spoke to me at the death of the child, of his statement that it ought not to be, that goodness, joy, hope, ought not to be, that it should be taken back, that one must take it back! "Ah, it ought not be!"—how those words stand almost like an instruction, a musical direction, set above the choral and instrumental movements of *The Lamentation of Dr. Faustus* and contained within every measure and cadence of this "Ode to Sorrow"! There is no doubt that he wrote it with an eye to Beethoven's Ninth, as its counterpart in the most melancholy sense of the word. But it is not merely that more than once it performs a formal negation of the Ninth, takes its back into the negative, but in so doing it is also a negation of the religious—by which I cannot mean its denial. A work dealing with the Tempter, with apostasy, with damnation—how can it be anything but a religious work? What I mean is an inversion, an austere and proud upending of meaning, such as I at least find, for example, in the friendly appeal by Dr. Faustus to the companions of his final hour that they should go to bed, sleep in peace, and be not troubled. Given the framework of the cantata, one can scarcely help viewing this as the conscious and deliberate reversal of the "Watch with me!" of Gethsemane. And again, his last drink with his friends . . . has all the marks of ritual, is presented as another Last Supper. Linked with this, however, is the reversal of the notion of temptation, in that Faust refuses the idea of salvation as itself a temptation—not only out of formal loyalty to the pact and because it is "too late," but also because with all his soul he despises the positive optimism of the world to which he is to be saved, the lie of its goodness. (514)

What Serenus says next, before his final paragraph of reading this composition, I want to underscore that while we and the author can see its appropriateness to him, especially in light of what he will soon say, it appears that he knows not what he says, as is fitting for the lover when speaking about his beloved:

This [rejection of cheap optimism] becomes even clearer and is still more forcefully elaborated in the scene with the good old 'physician and gossip' who invited Faust to him in a pious attempt at conversion and whose role is quite purposefully drawn as that of a tempter. This is an unmistakable reference to Jesus' temptation by Satan, just as an '*Apage!*' [Be gone!] is unmistakably found in the proudly despairing 'No!' spoken against false and flabby bourgeois piety. (514–15)

The final paragraph of the penultimate chapter is justifiably famous and deserves to be quoted in full:

> But yet another final, truly final reversal of meaning must be recalled here, must be pondered with the heart, a reversal that comes at the end of this work of endless lament and that, surpassing all reason, softly touches the emotions with that spoken unspokenness given to music alone, I mean the cantata's last orchestral movement, in which the chorus loses itself and which sounds like the lament of God for the lost state of His world, like the Creator's sorrowful "I did not will this." Here, toward the end, I find that the uttermost accents of sorrow are achieved, that final despair is given expression, and—but I shall not say it, for it would mean a violation of the work's refusal to make any concessions, of its pain, which is beyond all remedy, were one to say that, to its very last note, it offers any other sort of consolation than what lies in expression itself, in utterance—that is to say, in the fact that the creature has been given a voice for its pain. No, to the very end, this dark tone poem permits no consolation, reconciliation, transfiguration. But what if the artistic paradox, which says that expression, the expression of lament, is born out of the construct as a whole, corresponds to the religious paradox, which says that out of the profoundest irredeemable despair, if only as the softest of questions, hope may germinate? This would be hope beyond hopelessness, the transcendence of despair—not its betrayal, but the miracle that goes beyond faith. Just listen to the ending, listen with me: One instrumental group after the other steps back, and what remains as the work fades away is the high G of a cello, the final word, the final sound, floating off, slowly vanishing in a *pianissimo fermata*. Then nothing more. Silence and night. But the tone, which is no more, for which, as it hangs there vibrating in the silence, only the soul still listens, and which was the dying note of sorrow—is no longer that, its meaning changes, it stands as a light in the night. (515)

So our question is, how should we read this final turn of the screw, this hope beyond hopelessness? Is it what the remarks about flabby bourgeois piety and optimism promised might come? Or is it the final gift of love by the narrator, that philologist, amateur player of the viola d'amour, and lifelong if sometimes lacking friend, who creates here his palely shining music of our night?

In conclusion, I have to confess that I am unhappy with the term "absolute irony," for it seems to collapse back into modernism a text halfway out of it, on its way to postmodernism, so to speak. It also draws it back even further, into the view of German romantic irony characterized and criticized by Hegel as "infinite absolute negativity," something that Kierkegaard in his master's thesis, *The Concept of Irony*, elaborated and practiced, ironically enough, at considerable length so as to incorporate both ends of the philosophical tradition that he faced at the time, Socrates and Hegel himself. Then, too, as I describe its action, absolute irony sounds like a precursor to deconstruction—the systematic disruption of all system formation by interrupting permanently the establishment of a dialectical logic of binary oppositions leading progressively to synthesis, whether final or provisional. So how should I see *Doctor Faustus* working via its ironic—(self-) parodic?—practice of parallel formations? I would like to be able to think about it, with a good conscience, in terms of physics, of physical systems, even entanglement, perhaps. But I am no expert in physics and so what I am about to say, which is very rough and preliminary, especially as a conclusion, may be nothing more than the familiar case of the humanist being a dilettante in science. If so, please forgive me my Faustian strain showing.

Erotic irony occurs, you recall, when the lover pays homage to the beauty of the beloved by sacrificing mind, reason, good sense, good judgment, and so on, a result nature is said to ecstatically enjoy. Let us think of this not in imaginative, aesthetic, or, certainly, moral terms but in terms of "energetics"—that is, in terms of how physical systems work. When a positively or negatively charged particle, say, an electron, leaps from one higher energy state to another, lower state, a burst of detectable energy is given off. The law of the conservation of energy requires this and requires that the amounts involved are parallel, balanced out, in both the equations and reality alike. So the greater the charges involved, the higher the initial energy state of the particle, and the lower and so the further the leap, the greater the resultant pop of power. Given the weight of literary and cultural history in *Doctor Faustus*, it may not be too far-fetched to think of its "absolute irony," put so powerfully into play with that history, then, on this analogy of "energetics," as if this textual gift of love were a virtual atomic bomb of love. But maybe *Doctor Faustus* is just one candle in the night, cursing the darkness, after all?

As you ponder these different alternatives, interrupting permanently but, I would hope, never simply arresting the dialectic of development and *Bildung*, I have two words for you, which probably work best, for all the ghosts in earshot, if they are now sung—contrapuntal glissando no doubt optional: "parallel formations"![18]

CHAPTER 3

Deus sive Natura

Avatars of the Creative Reader in *Lolita*

MY RELATIONSHIP TO *Lolita* (1955; 1958) has not been an easy one. I chose not to read it in the 1960s when I first heard about it because of its subject matter (pedophilia, kidnapping, murder) and because it was already such a controversial success as a cultural icon ("You've read the book, now see the Stanley Kubrick movie!") among the intellectual class to which I then aspired. I preferred, like my perennial hero Nietzsche, never to join the winning side, which doesn't mean I always join the other, losing side either. Sometimes it means that, like him, I just wait, sitting it out, watching or ignoring the parade as it passes me by, which is what I did with this mid-century, modern classic novel whose narrator describes himself as an artist and a madman, "a murderer with a fancy prose style."[1] And his double in all things, Clare Quilty, is both a semi-successful playwright and a pedophile with whom a desperate Dolores Haze ("my Lolita," as Humbert repeatedly calls her throughout) manages her escape, only to be pressed into pornographic films, which when she resists, gets her thrown out of Quilty's ersatz Gothic, libertine mansion. This is what was meant way back then by "literature"? I thought not. Pulp fiction, maybe. . . .

Similarly, with the rest of its author's celebrated oeuvre: just so many too-clever-by-half traps. Nabokov was just too famous for his self-conscious ironies, his reflexively elaborate games, his buried traps for the reader, all those largely parodic allusions—topical, literary, and cultural; elite and popular—and the repeatedly cited pastiches of conventional structures, forms, discourses, fictional scenes, styles.[2] Although I had read—twice, with lots of guide-books—Joyce's *Finnegans Wake,* and despite knowing Nabokov's special disdain for this last work and even later portions of *Ulysses,* I felt his methods were just a continuation of late Joycean tricks to the point where they were completely hollowed-out, mere magician's sleights of hand, empty gestures made without any passion, and who needs that? In short, having read all about the would-be enchanter Nabokov at the time, like any good college sophomore, I formed my opinion in cement on the basis of no experience and was stuck in it.

Then, in my first semester (fall 1976) as an assistant professor at Princeton University, I was assigned to teach one of the breakout sections (a "preceptorial," in Princeton lingo) of a lecture course on the modern American novel being taught by an advanced assistant professor, Dorothy Klopf. (Thanks, Dorothy.) So, during the summer before I started, I read or reread all of the texts for the course, having gotten the syllabus in advance, eager-beaver that I was. Or maybe just frightened rabbit?

I found that I liked *Lolita,* despite all my ignorant expectations. To me at that time the pedophilia ("pederosis" in Humbert's neologism, 55) was not the point but the inhumanity of the narrator's lust. I was such a simple young man then. What I certainly did not believe was that the novel was about its reflexive metafictional games—these were intellectual equivalents of the pornographic passages—which were hardly that even by mid-century standards—for its audiences: different bait for different readers.

One thing crystal clear to me then too was that the authentic European high culture was being represented by a mere would-be genius, a manqué-man as Humbert virtually calls himself (one of many "manqué talents," 15), an ersatz figure or, in one of our contemporary terms, a simulacrum. As I said, I was such a simple young man then. Lionel Trilling had spent his life warning against—and some unkind critics would say, exemplifying, despite himself—such bad faith sensibility. These folks have the imagination of genius but none of the genius, for either creativity or hard work.[3]

But the America represented—that was what I had lived through myself: it was the real thing, for sure—that is, the real phony, filled with all its authentic gimmicks, cons, fabrications, lies, brand X advertisings—plastics was its watchword. And what Humbert was, a cruel pedophile wannabe artist and madman (that too I took as fake), and what America was, as represented by its impact on Dolores Haze, his Lolita: was there really a dime's worth of difference between them as far as the genuine article was concerned? At the time I assimilated Nabokov to the neither/nor, plague on both your houses type of high modernist irony familiar from Joyce or in some moments Yeats and Forster. I had not yet learned that in a world of fakes the fake of however horrible sort at least cannot logically be called inauthentic.

Reading *Lolita* nearly thirty years later, and catching up on most of what has been written about it and its author since, I do not think the same way. Although I do not endorse single-mindedly his wife Vera Nabokov's 1978 statement that the otherworld (*Potustoronnost*) is "the main theme" in her husband's work, I think *Lolita,* like all his major texts, is designed as a humanistic heterocosm. In the introductions to both his *Lectures on Don Quixote* and *Lectures on Literature,* for just two major instances, Nabokov begins by stressing that literary works are new or original worlds unto themselves, whose details are, if they are aesthetic masterpieces, uniquely selected and uniquely arranged, even perhaps singularly so.[4]

But at this point I hear advocates of the otherworld thesis objecting that this is a metafictional, while they intend a metaphysical, meaning to the word, although not necessarily an afterworldly one. Here is where I need to make some finer distinctions.

One of the key features of literature as an institution, no matter which critical theorist one consults, is that of the «system» it formed as it emerged with the rise of the bourgeois to power at the end of the eighteenth and beginning of the nineteenth century. And this system is based on the idea of the literary work of art as a heterocosm: an "organically" composed model of the world as it is and/or should be.[5] This literary system, both ideology and institution, comprises the means of production, circulation, evaluation, and reproduction of texts, commentaries, translations, editions, etc. Among its assumptions and justifying ideas is that the authors studied are geniuses, the works masterpieces; and these masterpieces produced by these geniuses, these "little worlds" unto themselves, depending on the genius and masterpiece under scrutiny, may correspond to, coincide with, or allusively symbolize the big world of either everyday reality or a higher reality, or even an intentional non-reality, a utopian or dystopian vision, depending on the case at hand. In sum, the literary system or institution is at bottom romanticism, as revised out of a certain strain or set of strains in early modern or renaissance writings. All later developments in literary history—realism, naturalism, symbolism, aestheticism, impressionism, imagism, modernism, postmodernism, etc.—are children of this literary system, often now returning home to the imperial capitals from the margins of former empires in further revised but still recognizable forms.

The literary system, in its emergence, has as its highest term usually not God but Nature, or in its later symbolist and post-symbolist variation, "anti-nature." Nature refers then to the proper operation of the literary system as it incorporates the life-works of its authors, scholars, critics, and, I suppose, its most devoted readers. And this proper operation? It is to produce visions of freedom in which individual voices compose a harmonious order, no matter how discordant any one voice may be, so that the norm of what it means to be human at the heart of the literary system may be passed on as cultural capital. And what is this norm? Ah, there's the rub. It of course varies from time to time, culture to culture, author to author, audience to audience, as they debate and revise in response to conditions.

I generally accept this argument about the literary system, although unlike Northrop Frye, I would not try to generalize from it to the entire verbal universe and make Blakean metaphysical claims.[6] Instead, I would turn to Spinoza to make claims about *Lolita* and the literary system as parts of one nature, one world. In Nabokovian terms, the otherworld for the creative reader is, and can only be, this world.

I know: Spinoza? If one says his name today, the likely response is to paraphrase something from Deleuze, his contemporary champion, and then say that post-structuralist stuff is all history now anyway.[7] But I want to argue that Spinoza is still viable for us once we return to him and read the *Ethics* for ourselves.[8] This is my experiment.

Spinzoa defines God, the mind (its origin and nature), human bondage to emotions, the power of the intellect or human freedom. None of what you might expect concerning these topics will you find in the pages of the *Ethics*. Yes, "the intellectual love of God" is the highest value, but what Spinoza means by that is something else again. But I need to focus on only a few things for my purposes here.

The famous, indeed infamous, phrase drawn from this posthumously published book is *"Deus, sive Natura,"* God or Nature. Since it was the seventeenth century, one understands why these were fighting words. For Spinoza, God or Nature refers in two different ways to the one substance that is the infinite universe and everything in it. God (to simplify my exposition, I will usually say "God" in what follows, except when I want to stress a point, so please also understand "or Nature" or that I am being pointed) has two infinite attributes, à la Descartes no doubt: extension and thinking. The mind and the body of human beings are finite versions of God. What is more, the mind is the idea of the body the body forms, even as the body and the mind cannot directly affect each other causally. The chain of causation of the mind and that of the body are separate but can indirectly affect each other via the ideas arising about each. All actions of the mind, of the body, are determined by causes, even if we do not know what they may be, and our ideas about them are confused and fragmentary, not clear and distinct—terms Spinoza again takes over from Descartes. It was the times. The freedom we have is that of learning what those causes (all modes or affections of God) specifically are and of producing our own appropriate cause to affect it and its effects. In this Spinoza, then, knowledge is naturally the highest value, and since God is the source of the greatest knowledge, the intellectual love of God makes a lot of sense if we want to maximum our albeit limited or determinate freedom.

What are the kinds of knowledge we possess? Here is Spinoza:

1. From individual objects presented to us through the senses in a fragmentary [*multilate*] and confused manner without any intellectual order . . . and therefore I call such perceptions "knowledge from casual experience."

2. From symbols. For example, from having heard or read certain words we call things to mind and we form certain ideas of them similar to those through which we imagine things. . . .Both these ways of regarding things I shall in future refer to as "knowledge of the first kind," "opinion," or "imagination."

3. From the fact that we have common notions and adequate ideas of the properties of things. . . . I shall refer to this as "reason" and "knowledge of the second kind." Apart from these two kinds of knowledge, there is, as I shall later show, a third kind of knowledge,

which I shall refer to as "intuition." This kind of knowledge proceeds from an adequate idea of the formal essence of certain attributes of God to an adequate knowledge of the essence of things. (51)

So we possess three kinds of knowledge, according to Spinoza: 1) opinion or imagination, 2) reason, and 3) intuition. This tripartite division looks familiar to us from Kant, with his sensibility (including imagination), understanding, and reason, the last two names of which make things clearer. Spinoza means by reason what Kant means by understanding, namely, calculating, piecemeal or incremental reasoning (not to say rationalizing), the step-by-step ratio following the chains of cause and effect, and the logical anticipation of what must follow in the series of causes and effects; and he means by intuition what Kant means by reason, what Wordsworth calls imagination in its most exalted mood: the intuition of where we fit in the vision of God or Nature, which is like the sudden simultaneous vision of all the phases of a process in an instant, what Spinoza calls *sub species aeternitate*. The example Spinoza gives here to demonstrate that each kind of knowledge, based on the perception of, reasoning about, and intuition of proportions and ratios of numbers, is a complicated one, so I will chose another example he gives later, to illustrate a somewhat different point, but I will treat it as an instance in the Spinozian spirit of his more familiar geometrical method.

Here is the example:

The nature of a circle is such that the rectangles formed from the segments of its intersecting chords are equal. Hence an infinite number of equal rectangles are contained in a circle, but none of them can be said to exist except insofar as the circle exists, nor again can the idea of any one of these rectangles be said to exist except insofar as it is comprehended in the idea of the circle. (33)

Imagination, reasoning, and the intuition of the geometrical principles for the formation of circles, chords, and rectangles—all are nicely demonstrated in this one instance. To put it another way: We experience a world of chords and must construct the circle from our partial experiences, but at a certain point in our learning experience we intuit the whole—circle and chords generating and constituting each other and our experience. (It can also work vice versa.) We see that vision with a clarity and distinction and so a certainty as surely as we know any principle or law that exceeds the merely empirical collection of details. We become active, creative readers of the cosmos that we live in and are. What Spinoza performs in this example and in his text as a whole is the logic of such formations, per se. His *Ethics,* in other words, whatever its value as a contribution to philosophy—metaphysics, epistemology, ethics—is a major contribution to the aesthetics of textual production that will be enshrined in what is to come in literary and intellectual history. Thanks to its adoption, revision, and incorporation by Kant and Hegel in their influential work, Spinoza's life-work permeates the literary system from romanticism to postmodernism and beyond.

In claiming this, I want to underscore, I am not making a comment, critical or otherwise, on the validity of Spinoza's *Ethics.* I am not trying to reduce or deconstruct it, nor am I saying that it is an allegory of anything or that it prophetically surveys allegories to follow. What I am claiming is that Spinoza's *Ethics* formulates originally and most purely the logic of textual production carried out by the conventions of the literary system in work after work, text after text. It is an instance of what it outlines, as are the texts of the literary system to come. It is like the literary system's "schematics," which have now gone global, virtual, and viral on the Internet.

Here is Nabokov's intuition of such a logic of reading in a celebrated passage on the positional power of poetry taken from his revised autobiography, *Speak, Memory* (1951; 1967)

But then, in a sense, all poetry is positional: to try to express one's position in regard to the universe embraced by consciousness, is an immemorial urge. The arms of consciousness reach out and grope, and the longer they are the better. Tentacles, not wings, are Apollo's natural members. Vivian Bloodmark, a philosophical friend of mine, in later years used to say that while the scientist sees everything that happens in one point of time, the poet feels everything that happens in one point of time. Lost in thought, he taps his knee with his wandlike pencil, and at the same instant a car (New York license plate) passes along the road, a child bangs the screen door of neighboring porch, an old man yawns in a misty Turkestan orchard, a granule of cinder-gray sand is rolled by the wind on Venus, a Docteur Jacques Hirsch in Grenoble puts on his reading glasses, and trillions of other such trifles occur—all forming an instantaneous and transparent organism of events, of which the poet (sitting in a lawn chair, at Ithaca, N.Y.) is the nucleus. (218)

Vivian Bloodmark is, of course, an anagram of Vladimir Nabokov. The expansiveness and self-irony, even self-parody, as in Nietzsche's idea of "the buffoonery of an emotion," go hand in hand.[9] To Spinoza-ize Nietzsche, the energies of the body, in battling each other for expressive release, inspire opposing images of each other, seeking to subsume and arrange a hierarchy of forces under themselves. God (or Nature) is simply the generic name for whichever side wins the latest battle in this endless war of affects, passions, and their active self-imaginations. Sooner or later, Nietzsche reminds us, the new favorite "ass" takes the stage.[10] A momentary stay against confusion thus supervenes, with tragic or comic resonances and reverberations.

Spinoza outlines the lineaments of the new symbolic order of virtually infinite imaginaries. And Lacan's real, since I am on that roll now? If we remember that the mind is the body's idea of itself in action, then the following passage surely points to it:

> *The mind's intellectual love toward God is the love of God wherewith God loves himself not insofar as he is infinite, but insofar as he can be explicated through the essence of the human mind considered under a form of eternity. That is, the mind's intellectual love toward God is part of the infinite love wherewith God loves himself.* (157, italics Spinoza's)

Nabokov, again citing this "friend" (or himself), names the power of the poet to envision life performatively along similar lines: "cosmic synchronization" (218). And all God's children be poets, in principle. Whether we think back to Spinoza and his discussion of God (or Nature) as the one substance of the universe, or further back to the Stoics and their vision of Cosmic Reason, or forward again to Rousseau and his "sense of being" and Wordsworth and his "sense sublime of something far more deeply interfused," or forward still to later ironic writers, such as T. S. Eliot in "Preludes," or even the furthest forward for now to us, making our trivial entries, each one of us positionally a poet, probably, on Facebook or some other popular social networking site, the world expands ever outward, spiraling out from the nucleus of a notation to the whole of the inscribed universe—or so it seems.[11] "Self-love," as Oscar Wilde deconstructively opined (*avant la lettre* of Derrida or Lacan), "is the beginning of a life-long romance"—for *Deus sive Natura,* too, apparently. After such self-irony, self-parody, who needs them?

"A colored spiral in a small ball of glass, this is how I see my own life" (275). Again and yet again, the logic of the text unfolds outward with the blazon of *Deus sive Natura*—or their equivalents—at its invisible heart. This is so for the creative reader.

Nabokov celebrates what he calls "the creative reader."

The good reader is one who has imagination, memory, a dictionary, and some artistic sense—which sense I propose to develop in myself and in others whenever I have the chance. Incidentally, I use the word reader very loosely. Curiously enough, one cannot read a book: one can only reread it. A good reader, a major reader, an active and creative reader is a rereader. And I shall tell you why. When we read a book for the first time the very process of laboriously moving our eyes from left to right, line after line, page after page, this complicated physical work upon the book, the very process of learning in terms of space and time what the book is about, stands between us and artistic appreciation. When we look at a painting we do not have to move our eyes in a special way even if, as in a book, the picture contains elements of depth and development. The element of time does not really enter in a first contact with a painting. In reading a book, we must have time to acquaint ourselves with it. We have no physical organ (as we have the eye in regard to a painting) that takes in the whole picture and then can enjoy its details. But in a second, or a third, or fourth reading we do, in a sense, behave towards the book as we do towards a painting. However, let us not confuse the physical eye, that monstrous achievement of evolution, with the mind, an even more monstrous achievement. A book, no matter what it is—a work of fiction or a work of science (the boundary line between the two is not as clear as is generally believed)—a book of fiction appeals first of all to the mind. The mind, the brain, the top of the tingling spine, is, or should be, the only instrument used upon a book. (3–4)

Such a creative reader would be able to see, as in the sense of Spinoza's third kind of knowledge, that *Speak, Memory* repeatedly anticipates in partial forms the final form of the vision of "cosmic synchronization" we discussed previously. Of course, not in a solemn spirit, but with ludic excess, as is Nabokov's wont. Similarly, the creative reader would see the same repeated partial anticipation of the vision concluding *Lolita* that Nabokov singles out in his famous afterword as containing the humanistic moral of the novel. Before turning to those passages, however, I want to spell out, based on Nabokov's broad hints in this passage, who is the creative reader par excellence.

Clearly—and distinctly!—the creative reader, the good reader, is first of all the author himself:

> The good reader is one who has imagination, memory, a dictionary, and some artistic sense—which sense I propose to develop in myself and in others whenever I have the chance. (3)

The author of the text is like Spinoza's God—or Nature!—in his cosmic vision of things by virtue of working through the imagination of sensuous details to a step-by-step rereading that follows the logic of the text's unfolding to a simultaneous intuition of the principle, the rule, of this text's formation. So too the good reader, the creative rereader is all of us—potentially, in our avatar guises as *Deus sive Natura,* following suit. I mean, ideally so, of course, that as with any regulative ideal supporting the intellectually loving norms of good reading, Nabokov himself in practicing criticism strongly endorses and underwrites herein.

"On a Book Entitled *Lolita*" is now printed as an afterword to most editions of the novel, a total of some fourteen million sold as of a decade or so ago. And now we have Kindle or Nook or iPad with our *Lolita* on them as they are on our laps. The general aim of the novel, as of any literary work, is not, Nabokov classically stipulates, a moralizing message ("in tow") but an ethic of humane intellectual ecstasy:

> *Lolita* has no moral in tow. For me a work of fiction exists insofar as it affords me what I shall bluntly call aesthetic bliss, that is a sense of being somehow, somewhere, connected with other states of being where art (curiosity, tenderness, kindness, ecstasy) is the norm. (314–15)

That is, for the creative reader first of all, the author, the text is one substance existing in the dimensions of time and space like a world where aesthetic bliss in Nabokov's unfolding multifarious sense exists: the novel, fiction, literature is the otherworld. And if Spinoza should be right, it is the real world, too.

Here is Nabokov pointing out what he calls "the nerves of the novel" (316) which he rediscovers on rereading:

> Every serious writer . . . is aware of this or that published book of his as a constant comforting presence. Its pilot light is steadily burning somewhere in the basement and a mere touch applied to one's private thermostat instantly results in a quiet little explosion of familiar warmth. This presence, this glow of the book in an ever accessible remoteness is a most companionable feeling, and the better the book has conformed to its prefigured contour and color the ampler and smoother its glows. But even so, there are certain points, byroads, favorite hollows, that one evolves more eagerly and enjoys more tenderly than the rest of one's book. I have not reread Lolita since I went through the proofs in the spring of 1955 but I find it to be a delightful presence now that it quietly hangs about the house like a summer day which one knows to be bright behind the haze. (315–16)

I am not sure if the enjoyment recollected here is all that far in its lineaments from both Spinoza's intellectual love of God and Humbert's more extensively self-loving kind. Despite Nabokov's best intention, Freud pops up in our minds—okay, in my dirty mind. I suppose one could claim that Humbert Humbert reaching the climax to end all climaxes against Lolita's squirming thighs and left buttock on the couch in her house while mother Charlotte is at church is a demonic parody of Freud, Spinoza, and Nabokov's own joy. Being able to see many opposing things converging into one is something both Nabokov and Spinoza prize. But oh that last "punny" word—haze. (Lolita's given name, we recall with a minor jolt, is Dolores Haze.)

In any event, Nabokov proceeds in the rest of the passage to single out "the nerves of the novel," paying particular attention, by its climactic placement in the expansively spiraling series, to Humbert's vision in the valley:

> And when I thus think of Lolita, I seem always to pick out for special delectation such images as Mr. Taxovich, or that class list of Ramsdale School, or Charlotte saying "waterproof," or Lolita in slow motion advancing toward Humbert's gifts, or the pictures decorating the stylized

garret of Gaston Godin, or the Kasbeam barber (who cost me a month of work), or Lolita playing tennis, or the hospital at Elphinstone, or pale, pregnant, beloved, irretrievable Dolly Schiller dying in Gray Star (the capital town of the book), or the tinkling sounds of the valley town coming up the mountain trail (on which I caught the first known female of *Lycaeides sublivens* Nabokov). These are the nerves of the novel. These are the secret points, the subliminal co-ordinates by means of which the book is plotted. (316)

And plotted not so much for meta-fictional ironies, parodies, or the like, as for the aesthetic bliss Nabokov loves.

While Humbert sits in his car awaiting the police to catch up with him, he recalls suddenly the vision he suffers on a mountain road shortly after Lolita ran off with Quilty:

One day, soon after her disappearance, an attack of abominable nausea forced me to pull up on the ghost of an old mountain road that now accompanied, now traversed a brand new highway, with its population of asters bathing in the detached warmth of a pale-blue afternoon in late summer. After coughing myself inside out, I rested on a boulder, and then, thinking the sweet air might do me good, walked a little way toward a low stone parapet on the precipice side of the highway. Small grasshoppers spurted out of the withered roadside weeds. A very light cloud was opening its arms and moving toward a slightly more substantial one belonging to another, more sluggish, heavenlogged system. As I approached the friendly abyss, I grew aware of a melodious unity of sounds rising like vapor from a small mining town that lay at my feet, in a fold of the valley. One could make out the geometry of the streets between blocks of red and gray roofs, and green puffs of trees, and a serpentine stream, and the rich, ore-like glitter of the city dump, and beyond the town, roads crisscrossing the crazy quilt of dark and pale fields, and behind it all, great timbred mountains. But even brighter than those quietly rejoicing colors—for there are colors and shades that seem to enjoy themselves in good company—both brighter and dreamier to the ear than they were to the eye, was that vapory vibration of accumulated sounds that never ceased for a moment, as it rose to the lip of granite where I stood wiping my foul mouth. And soon I realized that all these sounds were of one nature, that no other sounds but these came from the streets of the transparent town, with the women at home and the men away. Reader! What I heard was but the melody of children at play, nothing but that, and so limpid was the air that within this vapor of blended voices, majestic and minute, remote and magically near, frank and divinely enigmatic—one could here now and then, as if released, an almost articulate spurt of vivid laughter, or the crack of a bat, or the clatter of a toy wagon, but it was all really too far for the eye to distinguish any movement in the lightly etched streets. I stood listening to that musical vibration from my lofty slope, to those flashes of separate cries with a kind of demure murmur for background, and then I knew that the hopelessly poignant thing was not Lolita's absence from my side, but the absence of her voice from that concord. (307–8)

Some of Nabokov's best commentators simply do not buy this climactic vision. Either Nabokov does not carry off Humbert's conversion, in a case of too much, too late, and all at once; or, given its position out of chronological order, this vision is too clever by half, clearly having special pleading designs on the reader—witness Humbert's campy direct address à la *Jane Eyre;* or it is too much of Nabokov shining through Humbert here and so fictional illusion is broken. I agree with this view, but the breaking of illusion is not done here in the interest of gamesmanship but of humanity, granting it as much to Humbert as to Dolores, by imaginatively presenting them, each in their own tragically meeting worlds, to the creative reader for critical judgment, as character, reader, and author coincide in an instant approximating, as best the finite can, the infinite, the divinely creative, visionary love.

For me, this vision is thus a case of "cosmic synchronization" if there ever was one. It is the unfolding point of the whole novel. Some of its evident pedigree: Rousseau's "sense of being" from *Reveries of a Solitary Walker;* any number of Wordsworthian visions; Blakean minute particles and fugitive creative moment; Emeronsian transcendental Genius or Nature; Paterian moments of the tragic dividing of forces in a person; Joycean epiphanies; Woolf's moments of being; Heidegger's moment of vision when the call of conscience repeats the subject's resolute commitment to its better angel; even Mallarmé's famous definition of poetic beauty as the perfect rose missing from all the bouquets (like that "first known female of *Lycaeides sublivens* Nabokov" from nature?); or pick one of your own. This is your literary institution at work. In mentioning these names, I may seem to be claiming too much for Nabokov or simply covering for the visions that I missed in Milton, Dante, the Bible, or some Russian classic: so be it!

What I propose is that we divide this vision between Humbert and his creator and best reader, much as Lionel Trilling does with Joyce and Gabriel Conroy in his commentary on the famous cosmic vision of the snow falling faintly through the universe on all the living and the dead at the end of "The Dead."[12] Joyce magnanimously grants his creature a share in this vision so that Conroy, not known previously in the story for his generosity of spirit or acute self-knowledge, may see and feel—at least to some degree—what Joyce sees and feels about the human condition and how best to respond to it, with "generous tears" for all concerned. I think the demonic fusion of Quilty and Humbert in the wrestling scene we have just read, in which the former is murdered by the latter, is comic preparation for what turns into an imaginative fusion of a higher kind, in which Humbert and Nabokov—and we fellow readers of "the friendly abyss"— become, after Humbert and we too perhaps, get over an acute case of Sartrean nausea, part of "one nature" (307)—or God. In perceiving imaginatively Spinoza's third kind of knowledge via Nabokov's "cosmic synchronization" of *Deus sive Natura,* the creative reader coincides moments at a time with the loftiest vision of human potential in this or any otherworld.

Lest this proposal appear too sentimental for any hardnosed critic, despite my subtle use of the Jesuitical double-truth, adapted from Averroes—hardly sentimentalist any of them—I also would like to suggest in conclusion that becoming, momentarily, avatars of the creative (re-) reader function in Nabokov's *Lolita, Deus sive Natura,* may sound less glamorous or sublime if we remember what kind of novel we are in—and what kind of pornographic scenes Clare Quilty appears to specialize in. Orgies would be Nabokov's old word; "cluster-fucks" would now be our brand-new one no doubt.

CHAPTER 4

Visionary Contact in the Interzone

On the Beat State in *Naked Lunch*

Gentle reader, we see God through our assholes in the flash bulb of
orgasm ... Through these orifices transmute your body ... The way OUT
is the way IN ...." (191)[1]

THESE LINES, a few pages from the end of the Atrophied Preface
attached to *Naked Lunch,* combine the major features of this anti-nov-
el's novel discourses.[2] As a would-be fictional memoir of the surreal and
visionary experiences in Tangier of its putative author, William Lee,
while taking the cure (yet again) for his addiction to heroin and other
substances, these lines cram together willy-nilly a handful of discursive
strains. The address to the reader, a century out of date, is knowing, hipster parody/pastiche, and yet, strangely as such, it is nonetheless being
used to convey the sincerely meant message that what follows should be
read as true advice in this explicitly self-advertised "how-to" book (in
the original introduction, 199–206). The seeing of God is the romantic
or transcendental "other level of experience" in danger of being totally
lost (187) to homogeneous barbaric trivialization in the post-war atomic
age of emergent worldwide consumerism. "The desecration of the human
image," which the novel both renders and focuses as "an assault upon the
reader," is an ultimately self-destructive desecration, ironically squared

(*Letters* 365). For we can thus see God now only via such a literally vile orifice due to the body's revolt against its oppressive normalization by a newly global, instrumental American culture, which knows as recognition of identity only the celebrity of its deviant sexualities. The mysticism of St. John Perse, as translated by T. S. Eliot's own late mysticism, is revised for this present occasion, just as the basic modernist techniques of ironic juxtaposition, cinematic montage, and collage-like mosaics of *The Waste Land* are put to use throughout this text's apparently randomly assembled collection of perversely surreal, vaudeville-like routines, as if Abbott and Costello were sadomasochistic, gay, and on junk—and two parts of the same psyche.

Beat attitude, ironically antique narrative gestures, modernist literary techniques, therapeutic guidebook point of view, sociological critique, tabloid and pornographic pop-cultural sensationalism, mystical visionary purposes, and intentionally obscene, even criminal (for the time) models of selfhood—all these elements knock against each other, never fusing into the usual seamless whole-cloth of the secondary revisionary lie à la the dream in Freud's famous analyses. *Naked Lunch* is closer to the raw dream-stuff than any other would-be fictional rendition of primary processes, despite (or because of?) its famously mediated composition by several hands and random events. And yet, it is most like a repeated lyric *cri du coeur* in which schizoid word salads are as likely as faux illiteracy.[3]

Brian Edwards usefully terms all this intentional debris or waste as a project for "disorienting the national subject" (158), a process of disruption and subversion that, as Edwards cites Deleuze as claiming, can produce the equivalent of a foreign language within language, "a grammar of disequilibrium" (158). Composed from letters and routines originally written to and for Allen Ginsburg, *Naked Lunch*, the quintessential instance of collective composition by Burroughs and his Beat buddies, Ginsburg, Kerouac, and others, produces its "grammar of disequilibrium" to disorient the Cold War American subject of the straight story, and linear narrative development, of facile binary oppositions, of McCarthyism and homophobia, of racism and sexism, in the interest of a vision of future possibility existing in a visionary now, a preposterous moment when the International Zone that is the multi-planed Tangier, or what Burroughs nicknames these many different Tangiers for diplomats, expatriate artists, cold warriors, nationalist and revolutionary native parties, and, back home, avid American consumers of popular media images of this most "notorious" city: "The Interzone." It hovers between its earlier administration by ten nations and its reincorporation into the new, independent Morocco. This period, roughly coinciding with Burroughs's continuous residence there (1954–57), extends his extraterritorial rights as an American in Tangier (his portable exceptionalism), even as it opens him to the potential violence against such Euro-American imperialist exploiters of hungry Arab boys for sex and to a growing understanding of possession by this spectral shadow that only this space beyond national or effective international control fosters. Tangier at this period is a haven for every form of investment speculation, criminal transgression, libertarian marketplace of desires, and revolutionary or utopian hopes. As such, despite its apparent differences, it prefigures remarkably our contemporary moments of fugitive breakdown in the global world system. *Naked Lunch,* in this context, is not only, or rather not primarily, a visionary epic in the tradition of Blake's *Jerusalem,* but also, or even more so, a visionary initiation that passes a last judgment, much as Blake's *Milton* does, upon all—including the recalcitrant dimension of the creative subject—that would block access to the imaginative sources of ethical knowledge and radical enlightenment. It is not simply, in other words, the U.S. national subject that *Naked Lunch* would disorient; it is that subject's parasitic existence in and fatalistically demonic possession of the would-be visionary writer William Burroughs that must be more than disoriented. It must be expelled and abjected, in its turn, within the innovative, multidimensional, and ceremonial spaces of Burroughs's savagely comic routines, his modern form of the medieval dream-vision psychomachia. This interstitial zone of judgment and self-judgment is what I mean by "the Beat State." It is multidimensional, equally external and internal conditionality, which inspires and supports, transiently to be sure, such transformative textual, personal, and political emergences exemplified by the creation of *Naked Lunch* and its universally singular triumph.

"'Possession' they call it . . . Sometimes an entity jumps in the body—outlines waver in yellow orange jelly—and hands move to disembowel the passing whore or strangle the nabor [*sic*] child in hope of alleviating a chronic housing shortage" (184). What Burroughs foregrounds in these lines is his latter-day version of the theory of genius. His is like Yeats's more famous theory: "I shall find the dark grow luminous, the void fruitful, when I understand I have nothing, that the ringers in the tower have appointed for the hymen of the soul a passing-bell." That is, it is modeled on rape, total if temporary usurpation of the host-body-psyche by what in the introduction to the 1985 publication of *Queer* he calls, thanks to Brion Gysin's coinage, "the ugly spirit" (xix). This spirit is attracted to the disintegrating mask of public persona. Due to passionate love or passionate addiction or really any expression of passion, Burroughs sees the mask fall apart. And like a ghost attracted to the blood of the sacrificed sheep in the fosse at the entrance to Hades in Homer's *Odyssey*, the daemonic being enters and possesses the writer, wholly, not only to inspire writing but even more to act out in the world, to lead from the performance of one routine or another, in a bar or at a party, to the fulfillment of destructive intentionality—whether writer's, victim's, daemon's, or all of them at once combined.

At best, the writer can hope to patrol the perimeters to ward off potential invaders and to monitor and prevent, if possible, potential acting out. Burroughs learns to do this from the accidental death of his wife, Joan Vollmer, who died when they attempted to do a William Tell routine, with Burroughs shooting a glass of champagne off her head with his 45 revolver. This blood sacrifice, Burroughs claims here, inadvertently made him into a writer, for by thereafter having to channel his routines into writing, he also learned to write his way out of complete domination by the ugly spirit so that he could discover the gentle reader of his would-be audience and muse—at first particular potential love-partners, Lewis Marker and Allen Ginsberg, and then generalized to his readership at large. A gentle reader would vanquish the ugly spirit via the gift of inspiration.

Burroughs, in his letters and journal-entries attributed to his writer-surrogate William Lee, thinks he discovers via analysis and his imaginative memoir writing the traumatic origins of his troubled gay subjectivity—split between self-acceptance and self-loathing—in his being made to perform oral sex, when a toddler, on his nanny Mary's boyfriend. Then again when three years old, and being forced by an older boy to do the same, he bites down hard on the latter's penis, getting a delayed revenge and causing a tempest in the household, or so he remembers it.

Of course, it would be too easy to see *Naked Lunch* in light of any reductive analogy with these origins, as an act of revenge on straight society mounted (from the rear, as it were) by an aggressively Beat gay hipster. But to feel even a touch assaulted by *Naked Lunch* is to feel, I think, what the Ugly Spirit, as channeled by Burroughs, intends the Gentle Reader to feel, thereby establishing authentic "contact," a word that, in all its possible senses, is the signal guide to the value system Burroughs maintains throughout his life-work.

To understand why this situation arises, however, we do not need to repeat well-known biographical or historical facts. Rather, we need to understand the rather neglected crisis in the literary system that *Naked Lunch* instances. Basically, this crisis can best be expressed in a question—what is it that we know when we know a work of literature? Is it an ideological illusion perpetrated by the bourgeois upon the rest of us in support of their life-world? Is it a more human form of understanding than natural or social sciences can give us? If so, to what extent is it different from knowledge of the deceptions and self-deceptions human beings are heir to? What positive knowledge, moral or otherwise, beyond the world-wise reinforcement of a radical skepticism, does literature as a cultural institution and practice grant us readers? Is the knowledge that we gain only knowledge of ourselves as members of some identity group or other? Or if it is knowledge of general human nature, as traditionally contended, how is it different from what we learn elsewhere more readily via a more rigorous and disciplined method? Surely the Kinsey Reports on human sexuality give greater knowledge of American sexual practices than literature has done up until that time. In short, the literary system, and especially the novel, were at the time being challenged and made to seem outmoded not only by modern popular media, such as photography, movies, radio, and TV, but by the inability to provide a serious defense of literature as anything other than socially sanctioned imaginary play therapy, essentially no better than pipedreams, for real problems. Although Burroughs asserts repeatedly that his routines, like dreams, could break into reality at any time, just as any reality could pass into the dream-world to become enlarged and transfigured there, what *Naked Lunch* demonstrates, more than this claim, is that knowledge that literature grants us, for better and for worse.

Such knowledge is the instantaneous intuition of all phases of the development of an entity, or, in the extreme-limit case of the idea of god, of the totality of entities. This intuitive knowledge is not derived from sense-data or from the operation of conceptual categories, but is generated in the discovery of the definitive principle for a being, or for the whole, at whatever level or scope. Just as we can determine the nature of the circle from the right angles, infinite in number, that constitute the circle's all possible chords, so too can we know the principle of development of a being, its rule or law, from the operation of our imagination of it. Like any other art at its best, literature in its respective fashion completes the draft of being. To paraphrase the romantic visionary terms of Wallace Stevens, from "Final Soliloquy of the Interior Paramour," we can say that the finite imagination of the text and the infinite imagination of god become one: the inherent emergent development of the literary system coincides in principle with a particular writer's singular composition. We can see the nature of the expressive future. What *Naked Lunch* reveals emerging is the fatally mad collective mind of full-blown consumer culture. It is the fictional memoir of its conception, gestation, birth, and death throes, composing an intellectual and emotional complex, an iconic cultural image, all presented in an instant of time. In saying this, I mean to underscore the essentially modernist project of *Naked Lunch*, even as it presents a vision of the divine perhaps more appropriate to the postmodernist nightmares of Jacques Lacan commenting on the god of the psychotic Dr. Schreber.

In fact, Schreber's god has a lot in common with the most bizarre characteristics of *Naked Lunch*. Long, protoplasmic tendrils or tentacles of light grope the soul and impregnate the receptive subject ready to give birth to the new messiah. The latter is to save us from the end of the world apocalypse that has just happened all because one morning, while dressing, Schreber has thought it might be nice to be a woman, having more pleasure than any man can have. It is as if Schreber's vision completes that of Burroughs.

From a Lacanian perspective, God, whether Schreber's or any other's, is the conventional name for the Big Other, that illusory other of the other and ourselves, the Father, who ensures the threat of castration so that the socially symbolic system of signification works from gender division on up the ladder. And it would be interesting to speculate that the invasive God of Burroughs is modeled upon what he comes to believe is his first traumatic experience of the adult world: his sexual abuse as a toddler by his nanny and her boyfriend. One could conclude that his early personal experience happens to coincide in some important ways with the widespread psychic effects of the U.S. population during the decade or so after World War II as the multimedia assault upon people to change them into consumers so that they then will buy, buy, buy kicks into high gear.

However this may be, there are clearly differences between the literary vision of Burroughs and the paranoid fantasies of Schreber, not least the formal intentional differences between literature and madness. But the vision of god—whether explicitly owned up to or not, or rationally argued for via geometric models and analogies à la Spinoza, or enthusiastically embraced via drugs and debauchery à la Burroughs— does express the norm of maximal energy or power that the subject can enjoy. The god of the subject is, of course, the superego writ large; and, in the case of the representative artist of a culture, assuming that there still may be such creatures, it also coincides at most points with the cultural superego. That we live now in an age of polytheism may be no improvement, however, on the theory that more means a dispersal of intensity; for it may just mean we have many more raging madnesses to evade than ever before.

Intuition is usually thought to be a non-rational mode of knowledge, if it is thought to be knowledge at all. For Spinoza, there is nothing non-rational about it. Rather, it is the mind's immediate perception of a principle of formation at work, like that (as we have seen) of the generation of a circle of a certain size from the specific dimensions of a right angle to be inscribed within it that produces its chords. This geometrical or axiomatic knowledge is Spinoza's favorite instance of the universal knowledge of how rules of combination and differentiation create forms of thinking and acting upon the world. It is intuitive knowledge of the mind at work. It is the mind's loving self-imagination in the moment of creation.[4] Burroughs's fascination with Sufism can be seen in this light.

Similarly, Burroughs's routines, begun to make and keep in contact with prospective beloveds (among others), evolve into techniques of discovery, both of the self and of its more general models of humanity, and so in this way at least instances the intellectual love of god, to put the matter in Spinoza's terms. For the self-loathing queer junky Burroughs, whose routine of playing William Tell with his wife led to her death, such a sublimated use for the routine demonstrates how becoming a writer of routines saved him, not to mention others, perhaps. But the cost of this intuitive or imaginative knowledge of the mind at work can be, as it is for Burroughs, great.

"Interzone," an article originally written for *The New Yorker* (it was never accepted), suggests as much in its characterization of Brinton, an American living in Tangier before full Moroccan independence in the mid-1950s who is, like William Lee, an ironic version of Burroughs:

Some of these men have ability and intelligence, like Brinton, who writes unpublishably obscene novels and exists on a small income. He undoubtedly has talent, but his work is hopelessly unsalable. He has intelligence, the rare ability to see relations between disparate factors, to coordinate data, but he moves through life like a phantom, never able to find the time, place or person to put anything into effect, to realize any project in terms of three-dimensional reality. He could have been a successful business executive, anthropologist, explorer, criminal, but the conjuncture of circumstances was never there. He is always too late or too early. His abilities remain larval, discarnate. He is the last of an archaic line, or the first here from another space-time way—in any case a man without context, of no place and no time. (50)

Some of this is self-serving, of course, which is why Burroughs assigns it to his new mask Brinton, not even giving it to Lee, who is too recognizably himself. But there is also real insight here. Burroughs, like the modern or post-romantic writer or artists generally, suffers from irony as a condition of death-in-life. Abstracted and alienated from his actual historical position in space-time, the modern artist like Burroughs is a principle of possibility, too early or too late, without context, of no place and no time. Why? Because he can see the full development of a thing, a career, a way of life, and so can never be fully in it. Which is what makes him like the last of a kind or the first of a new alien breed. The modern artist, like Burroughs, is a caesura, a hiatus, more than anything else, a hole in reality. Like the figure in *Naked Lunch* of the Buyer (a narc who needs the junk he buys to make his busts), or like the junk itself in this text when personified as driven living capital, Burroughs as ironic modern artist is most of all "a creature without species" (17), and thus, in his art, the visionary perception incarnate of the principle of species-making. The intuitive knowledge of all that he lacks by way of determinant formation gives Burroughs then access to the actual templates of being—which is why he can play comic, pornographic, nihilistic, and unspeakable variations on the normal or proper—but also lyrical—paeans to love.

The centerpiece of *Naked Lunch* and what many critics refer to as its Bataillean "general" or "anal" economy is of course "the talking asshole routine" (110–13). Originally the tail end of a letter to Ginsberg, meant to amuse and entice him, in revised form it ends up in the "Ordinary Men and Women" chapter of the novel. Drs. Schafer and Benway—the latter Burroughs's spokesman for modern medicine gone wild in its experimentation and drive to help control the population—are discussing absurd ways to surgically remake the human body to make it more efficient in its functioning—recreating form to perfect its function: "Why not one all-purpose blob?" (110). Benway suddenly recalls the story of "the man who taught his asshole to talk" (110).

> This ass talk had a sort of gut frequency. It hit you right down there like you gotta go. You know when the old colon gives you the elbow and it feels sorta cold inside, and you know all you have to do is turn loose? Well this talking hit you right down there, a bubbly, thick stagnant sound, a sound you could *smell*. (110–11)

Benway goes on to explain that the man worked for a carnival and treated his talking asshole as part of a novelty ventriloquist act, which fits nicely with the passage above, as ventriloquism is originally a religious practice in ancient Greece called gastromancy, or "speaking from the stomach," or in this case, the colon!

The act at this point sounds most like minstrel show routines, such as

> "Oh, I say, are you still down there, old thing?"
> "Nah! I had to go relieve myself." (111)

But then the asshole starts talking on its own, ad-libbing and tossing back gags at the straight-man ventriloquist every time. It gets worse, Benway says, when the asshole develops teeth-like "little raspy incurving hooks" and starts eating. At first the man thinks this is cute and funny, but then the asshole begins to eat its way through his pants, exposing him in public, shouting on the street that it wants "equal rights" (111), getting drunk and having crying jags, saying "nobody loved it" and all it wanted is to be kissed "same as any other mouth" (111). Finally, the asshole talks "all the time day and night," with the man shouting for it to shut up, beating it with his fist, "sticking candles up it" (to curse the darkness, I guess). Then one day the asshole says to him, "'It's you who will shut up in the end. Not me. Because we don't need you around here any more. I can talk and eat *and* shit'" (111).

After that [the man] began waking up in the morning with a transparent jelly like a tadpole's tail all over his mouth. This jelly was what the scientists call un-D.T., Undifferentiated Tissue, which can grow into any kind of flesh on the human body. He would tear it off his mouth and the pieces would stick to his hands like burning gasoline jelly and grow there, grow anywhere on him a glob of it fell. So finally his mouth sealed over, and the whole head would have amputated spontaneous—(did you know there is a condition occurs in parts of Africa and only among Negroes where the little toe amputates spontaneously?)—except for the *eyes,* you dig. That's one thing the asshole *couldn't* do was see. It needed the eyes. But nerve connections were blocked and infiltrated and atrophied so the brain couldn't give orders any more. It was trapped in the skull, sealed off. For a while you could see the silent, helpless suffering of the brain behind the eyes, then finally the brain must have died, because the eyes *went out,* and there was no more feeling in them than a crab's eye on the end of a stalk. (111–12)

Dr. Benway's mad tale has the routine coming full circle, now reaching the point of intersection with Dr. Schafer's original demonic parody of a visionary proposal to alter the inefficient human body into something resembling a giant eel: "Instead of a mouth and an anus to get out of order why not have a one all-purpose hole to eat *and* eliminate? We could seal up nose and mouth, fill in the stomach, make an air hole direct into the lungs where it should have been in the first place . . ." (110). But the routine continues, not closing, but opening up to three new themes: 1) how sex leaks out of even the least sexy of our communications; 2) how modern democracy is really a fatal virus of bureaucracy, a deadly parasite in the body politic; and 3) finally, on a lighter note, as it were, how love perhaps does conquer even the asshole in us all.

Oliver Harris has shown that the first of these new themes, how sex leaks out of every pore in the body of communication, is originally in the letter where this routine is hatched. In that epistolary context, it is in the first, not one of the final, positions. It all fits better there. But in this novelistic context, one wonders how sex leaking out of even the least of our communications, squeezing pass the censor bureaus, quite works—I mean, beyond the very general and obvious sense that the routine deals with the body and does end with a surreal scene of anal sex. As a reference to the passage about the Undifferentiated Tissue, it is not clear how it works, at first.

I think what Burroughs means, however, goes beyond any general and obvious points. His story about the asshole that talks, wants equal rights, is subject to drunken crying jags when neglected, develops vicious teeth in a parody of the *vagina dentata*, is his version of Milton's and the Bible's creation of Eve, adjusted for either straight or queer application. Instead of the feminine being born of the rib of the masculine, it is born of the anus.

Similarly, the idea of modern democracy as a deadly parasite, a fatal virus like a cancer of bureaucracy, is Burroughs's revision of the myth of modern democracy as a direct descendant of the Athenian political system. Rather, because of the censorship of sex, especially in its homo-erotic forms, modern bureaucratic democracy, especially in its drive for mastery and control of the population, represents the end of the human species as we have known it—hence, the sci-fi degeneration and devolution where one might have expected or hoped for mutation to the next rung on the evolutionary ladder. The homosocial dimension of modern democracy, long recognized but also usually repressed except in certain rare instances, such as that of Whitman's poetry, gives rise in the context of the repression of the 1950s to the nightmare scenarios in the novel, as well as in the culture at large. The final new theme, of comical but also quite loving, sexuality, in this instance appropriately homoerotic and anal, is the necessary sign from Burroughs's Ugly Spirit for the Gentle Reader to pay heed, as Blake says in *Milton,* to mark his words as they are of our eternal salvation. Burroughs in *Naked Lunch* revises—satirically, parodi-cally, and creatively (I will argue)—the Judeo-Christian and classical cul-tural legacies of the Western tradition.

Burroughs, however, is also a legatee of that tradition's most virulent "diseases" of misogyny and misanthropy, with strong taints of racism and Orientalism, and even (especially given the historic immediacy of the Holocaust) anti-Semitism. Burroughs ironically puts everything into the mouths of characters or the author-surrogates in the novel, and hence much of what passes his lips in these crazed routines remains open to considerable debate. To put it another way, as the self-appointed Anus of the Western World (Joyce was only Ireland's), we know that in reading Burroughs we are going to get dirty, to say the least. This abjection of the reader is of course a large part of his authorial intention, especially in *Naked Lunch.* The first time I read an excerpt from it in *Evergreen Review* a half century ago, I gagged and buried the magazine in an old wooden chest my father had made for his gear when in the Navy during World War II. It had been turned into a toy chest and then was the depository for old magazines. At age twelve this reader's sensibility felt ravaged. But this is the point I now realize. More than a deal with the devil, more than a pedophile's love-letter to his lost love(s), *Naked Lunch* is that rare thing, a book that probably is really obscene, filled with what Burroughs calls "the Ugly Spirit" hunting down to destroy the last vestiges of innocence in any "Gentle Reader" who falls into the traps of its demonic routines. Force the American Readers to face the worst of what their existences presume everyday as preconditions. As the cherry on top of this heap of messy word-salad sundaes, add the self-loathing expressions of a junky queer from the U.S. heartland (in every sense), who finds every vicious underground from around the miserable world of the 1950s. And as radical cure for maniacal consumerism, *Naked Lunch*'s imaginary dripping fork in pure waste has now virtually global reach: "The title means exactly what the words say: **NAKED** Lunch—a frozen moment when everyone sees what is on the end of every fork" (199).

Benway's conclusion to the "Talking Asshole" routine may at first continue in the same hard-edged, cynically brutal vein, but it suddenly ends with a new tone and perspective:

> In Timbuktu I once saw an Arab boy who could play a flute with his ass, and the fairies told me he was really an individual in bed. He could play a tune up and down the organ hitting the most exogenously sensitive spots, which are different on everyone, of course. Every lover had his special theme song which was perfect for him and rose to his climax. The boy was a great artist when it came to improvising new combines and special climaxes, some of them notes in the unknown, tie-ups and seeming discords that would suddenly break through each other and crash together with a stunning, hot sweet impact. (113)

Underneath all the obvious crudity in this passage, Benway reports on an imaginative perception about the nature of virtuosity in love-making (taken from "fairies"). This sharp intuition rises to a plausible generalization about the rare genius in the art of love. It is perhaps based upon Burroughs's own experiences in Tangier or Mexico, and so he identifies himself as in this flaming group of gay men. It also says something pertinent about the visionary writer's individualizing designs of aesthetic enjoyment. They are palpable upon the reader's body, but in an interpenetrative spirit, as is any other more recognizable form of *jouissance*. In other words, Benway is channeling Burroughs here, even as Burroughs may be channeling, at least for this masterfully comic vision of love at play, the transfigured memory of his own boy-lover Kiki. The Ugly Spirit and the Gentle Reader are, momentarily, reconciled.

How are we to understand this admittedly brief and unexpected vision of reconciliation in a novel that is perhaps the most indigestible of all? I think Spinoza's theory of conatus and its relation to the intellectual love of God may help us to understand Burroughs, as strange as that may sound.

"Conatus" is the term that Spinoza calls the activity of any being directed to its continuation in existence as the being it is. This activity in itself gives pleasure. Conatus is neither desire nor will, unless one sees it as a pleasuring or a willing that is in fact an acting to ensure a being's existence as such. "The highest conatus of the mind," Spinoza says, and the mind is the idea of the body that the body has of itself, and the mind's "highest virtue is to understand things by the third kind of knowledge" (154). That is, not by sensuous perception, nor by rational understanding, but by intuition. From this third kind of knowledge or intuition, the mind learns the intellectual love of God, which is Spinoza's end-all and be-all, as it defines the ultimate conatus of existence, of being rather than nothing.

> The mind's intellectual love toward God is the love of God wherewith God loves himself not insofar as he is infinite, but insofar as he can be explicated [in his attributes and their modes] through the essence of the human mind considered under a form of eternity. That is, the mind's intellectual love toward God is part of the infinite love wherewith God loves himself. (157)

Each region of being constitutes a divine attribute, of which we know two, the *res cognitans* and *res extenza*, the thinking thing and the extended thing, subject and object. The modes of these attributes are as many and different as there are entities in existence. The intellectual love of God is "of" him in two senses, then: both the love we feel toward God and the love God feels toward us and all that exists, that expresses its conatus. This view has gotten Spinoza accused of being a pantheist and notoriously excommunicated from the Jewish faith, as it would no doubt appall any monotheistic religionist, despite its being a rather curious pantheism:

there is one God, interchangeable with the Nature of modern science; that is, with the universe of matter and its laws. In any event, Spinoza's *Ethics* may well express the visionary's highest sense of virtue, which is why I find it useful in this context.

In conclusion, I would recall these programmatic words from "Islam Incorporated and the Parties of the Interzone," where there is a naked lunch menu printed out for the reader to assimilate. Without getting into the niceties of these different Interzone parties, the one Burroughs favors, the Factualists, has as its platform, in part, the following rejection of the use of telepathy, which was being investigated seriously at the time by U.S. and Soviet Union intelligence agencies for its potential mind-control power over its respective populations (at least):

> We oppose, as we oppose atomic war, the use of such knowledge to control, coerce, debase, exploit or annihilate the individuality of another living creature. Telepathy is not, by its nature, a one-way process. To attempt to set up a one-way telepathic broadcast must be regarded as an unqualified evil. . . . (140)

What Burroughs calls "The Human Virus" (141) is the coercive use of knowledge, as opposed to its free intellectual pursuit. The "Deteriorated Image" of the human species, the "broken image of Man moves in minute by minute and cell by cell," (141), like cancer, or junk, or self-loathing. But *"The Human Virus can be isolated and treated"* (141).

How? through God's love, of course:

> Gentle reader, we see God through our assholes in the flash bulb of orgasm . . . Through these orifices transmute your body . . . The way OUT is the way IN . . . . (191)

Thus saith the Divine Asshole? More "notes in the unknown" (113).

No wonder, then, that the creatively disjunctive discourses of Burroughs's genius-work of visionary imagination transforms with exuberant laughter the actual architecture and urban design of Tangier's central district into a cubist collage depicting the modern inferno as a gigantic Dadaist toilet bowl especially equipped with the monstrous sounds of infinite suction. An American Standard: Beat-Style, Beat-State.

Chapter 1

1. For useful books on genius and its ancient, romantic, and modern cultures, see: Jacques Derrida, *Geneses, Genealogies, Genres, and Genius: The Secrets of the Archive,* trans. Beverley Bie Brahic (New York: Columbia University Press, 2006); Phillipe Lacoue-Labarthe and Jean-Luc Nancy, *The Literary Absolute: The Theory of Literature in German Romanticism,* trans. Philip Barnard and Cheryl Lester (Albany: SUNY Press, 1988); Thomas McFarland, *Originality and Imagination* (Baltimore and London: The Johns Hopkins University Press, 1985); Penelope Murray, ed., *Genius: The History of an Idea* (Oxford: Blackwell, 1989); Gustavus Stadler, *Troubling Minds: The Cultural Politics of Genius in the United States, 1840–1890* (Minneapolis: University of Minnesota Press, 2006). For useful articles, see: Harold Bloom, "Clinamen, or Poetic Misprision," *New Literary History* 3.2: On Interpretation: I (Winter 1972): 373–91; David Bromwich, "Reflections on the Word Genius," *New Literary History* 17.1: Philosophy of Science and Literary Theory (Autumn 1985): 141–64; Jerome C. Christensen, "The Genius in the *Biographia Literaria,"* *Studies in Romanticism* 17.2 (Spring 1978): 215–31; C. S. Lewis, "Genius and Genius," *The Review of English Studies* 12.46 (April 1936): 189–94; Perry Miller, "Emersonian Genius and the American Democracy," *The New England Quarterly* 26.1 (March 1953): 27–44; Ralph Virtanen, "On the Dichotomy between Genius and Talent," *Comparative Literature Studies* 18.1 (March 1981): 69–90.

2. Lionel Trilling, *The Moral Obligation To Be Intelligent,* edited and with an introduction by Leon Wieseltier (New York: Farrar, Strauss and Giroux, 2000).

3. For a fuller discussion of this Trilling commentary, see my *Lionel Trilling: The Work of Liberation* (Madison: University of Wisconsin Press, 1988), pp. 238–42.

4. Lionel Trilling, *Prefaces to the Experience of Literature* (New York: Harvest Books, 1981).

5. James Joyce, *Dubliners: Critical Edition,* ed. Margot Norris (New York: Norton, 2006), pp. 311–12.

6. For essential books on Spinoza and his relationship to the issues raised here, see: Gilles Deleuze, *Expressionism in Philosophy: Spinoza,* trans. Martin Joughlin (New York: Zone Books, 1992); Steven Nadler, *Spinoza's Ethics: An Introduction* (New York: Cambridge University Press, 2006); Thomas McFarland, *Coleridge and the Pantheist Tradition* (Oxford at the Clarendon Press, 1969); Michael L. Morgan, ed., *The Essential Spinoza: Ethics and Related Writings,* trans. Samuel Shirley (Indianapolis and London: Hackett, 2006). For articles, see: Laura Byrne, "The Geometrical Method in Spinoza's *Ethics,*" *Poetics Today* 28.3 (Fall 2007): 441–74; F. C. Copleston, "Spinoza and Pantheism," *Philosophy* 21.78 (April 1946): 42–56; Michael Della Rocca, "Spinoza and the Metaphysics of Scepticism," *Mind* 116.464 (October 2007) 851–74; Fritz Kaufmann, "Spinoza's System as Theory of Expression," *Philosophy and Phenomenological Research* 1.1 (September 1940): 83–97; James C. Morrison, "Why Spinoza Had No Aesthetics," *The Journal of Aesthetics and Art Criticism* 47.4 (Autumn 1989): 359–65; Steven Nadler, "Spinoza and Consciousness," *Mind* 117.467 (July 2008): 575–601; Martha Nussbaum, "The Ascent of Love: Plato, Spinoza, Proust," *New Literary History* 25.4: 25th Anniversary Issue, Part 2 (Autumn 1994): 925–49; G. H. R. Parkinson, "Hegel, Pantheism, and Spinoza," *Journal of the History of Ideas* 38.3 (July–September, 1977): 449–59; Ralph C. Walker, "Spinoza and the Coherence Theory of Truth," *Mind New Series,* 94.373 (January, 1985): 1–18; Benjamin Wolstein, "The Romantic Spinoza in America," *Journal of the History of Ideas* 14.3 (June 1953): 439–50.

Chapter 2

1. All citations from the English version will be to Thomas Mann, *Doctor Faustus: The Life of the German Composer Adrian Leverrkuhn As Told by a Friend,* trans. John E. Woods (New York: Vintage, 1997) and hereafter given in the text.

2. I am, of course, referring to Fredric Jameson, but also to Alan Wilde and William V. Spanos, among others. For an interesting but opposing view on the oppositions in the novel, see Jameson, "Allegory and History: Rereading Doctor Faustus," *The Modernist Papers* (London: Verso, 2007), pp. 91–123.

3. R. P. Blackmur, *Eleven Essays in the European Novel* (New York: Harcourt, Brace & World, Inc., 1964). The chapter on *Faustus* is entitled suggestively "Parody and Critique."

4. Thomas Mann, *The Story of a Novel: The Genesis of Doctor Faustus,* trans. Richard and Clara Winston (New York: Knopf, 1961); Thomas Mann, *Reflec-*

tions of a Non-Political Man, trans. Walter D. Norris (New York: Fredrick Ungar, 1983), chapter 4.

5. See my *Radical Parody: American Culture and Critical Agency after Foucault* (New York: Columbia University Press, 1992), for further discussion of this topic.

6. Edward W. Said, *Musical Elaborations* (New York: Columbia University Press, 1991).

7. For an essential basic understanding of Western music, see J. Peter Burkholder et al., eds., *A History of Western Music,* 8th ed. (New York: W. W. Norton, 2010); Piero Weiss and Richard Taruskin, *Music in the Western World: A History in Documents,* 2nd ed., selected and annotated by Weiss and Taruskin (Belmont, CA: Schirmer Cengage Learning, 2008). For Schoenberg, see Arnold Schoenberg, *Theory of Harmony,* trans. Roy E. Carter (Berkeley and Los Angles: University of California Press, 1983). For the new music of the last century, see Theodore W. Adorno, *Philosophy of Modern Music,* trans. Anne G. Mitchell and Wesley V. Blomster (New York and London: Continuum, 2004).

8. For the German edition, see Thomas Mann, *Doktor Faustus* (Frankford am Main, Germany: S. Fischer Verlag, 2007). All citations to the German edition will be from this text. For the industrious, there is a supplementary volume of over 1,000 pages of critical annotations.

9. For *Death in Venice,* see Thomas Mann, *Stories of Three Decades,* trans. H. T. Lowe-Porter (New York: Knopf, 1936). Citations are from this text. There are other, new translations, but none yet by John E. Woods, the preferred English translator by far. Here is one of the most recent ones: Thomas Mann, *Death in Venice,* trans Michael Henry Heim, introduction by Michael Cunningham (New York: Harper/Collins, 2004).

10. The question of the novel's narrator is a greatly disputed matter. For summary judgments of these debates and all others associated with *Doctor Faustus,* see Michael Beddow, *Landmarks of World Literature: Thomas Mann, Doctor Faustus* (Cambridge: Cambridge University Press, 1994); John F. Fetzer, *Changing Perceptions of Thomas Mann's Doctor Faustus: Criticism 1947–1992* (Columbia, SC: Camden House, 1996); Frances Lee, *Overturning Doctor Faustus: Rereading Thomas Mann's Novel in Light of Observations of a Non-Political Man* (Rochester, NY: Boydell and Brewer, 2007).

11. Thomas Mann, "Freud and the Future," in his *Essays of Three Decades,* trans. H. T. Lowe-Porter (New York: Knopf, 1947), pp. 411–28. All citations are from this translation. For an excellent contemporary development of the utopian hopes for psychoanalysis in a more tragic humanistic vein, see Abraham Drassinower, *Freud's Theory of Culture: Eros, Loss, and Politics* (Lanham and New York: Rowan & Littlefield, 2003. Of course, Freud's theory of the death-instinct or drive is that an individual and a society can develop via the formation of a conscience as a pure culture of the death-instinct. What explanatory power such

a global theory has is greatly disputable. See Sigmund Freud, *Beyond the Pleasure Principle and Other Writings,* trans. John Reddick with an introduction by Mark Edumnson (New York: Penguin Books, 2003).

12. See Paul A. Bove, "Misprisions of Utopia: Messianism, Modernism, and Allegory," in a *Preface to Henry Adams* (Cambridge: Harvard University Press, 2011).

13. See Bove, "Misprisions."

14. http://dictionary.reverso.net/german-english/collins

15. Thomas Mann, *Doctor Faustus,* trans. H. T. Lowe-Porter (New York: The Modern Library, 1948), 306.

16. See Lee's and Fetzer's books cited above.

17. As to the question of the Diaries clearing things up, given their edited form in English at least, they are unlikely to settle anything. See Thomas Mann, *Diaries, 1918–1939,* selection and foreword by Hermann Kesten, translated by Richard and Clara Winston (London: Robin Clark, 1984). The two latest biographies in English are more helpful but still not definitive on this question. See Anthony Heilbut, *Thomas Mann: Eros and Literature* (Berkeley and Los Angeles: University of California Press, 1995); Hermann Kurzke, *Thomas Mann: Life as a Work of Art,* trans. Leslie Wilson (Princeton and Oxford: Princeton University Press, 2002).

18. I want to thank Gina MacKenzie, Michelle Martin, and Alan Singer for their comments on an earlier version of this chapter. I have been especially helped by Ms. Martin's comments and by her work on the modern novel and Georges Bataille's theory of "the accursed share."

Chapter 3

1. Vladimir Nabokov, *The Annotated Lolita,* revised and updated, ed. Alfred Appel, Jr. (New York: Vintage, 1991), p. 9. Hereafter all citations from this edition will be given in the text.

2. The Nabokov industry contributes mightily to this perception of their author, but it has also been wonderfully helpful. What follows are the list of books and articles most helpful to me:

Books: Vladimir E. Alexandrov, *Nabokov's Otherworld* (Princeton: Princeton University Press, 1991); Brian Boyd, *Vladimir Nabokov: The Russian Years* (Princeton: Princeton University Press, 1990); Brian Boyd, *Vladimir Nabokov: The American Years* (New York: Vintage, 1991); Julian W. Connolly, ed, *The Cambridge Companion to Nabokov* (New York: Cambridge University Press, 2005). (especially useful in these books are the essays by Brian Boyd, John Burt Foster, Jr., Ellen Pifer, and Susan Elizabeth Sweeney); Julian W. Connolly, ed., *A Reader's Guide to Lolita* (Boston: Academic Studies Press, 2009); Jane Grayson, Arnold

McMillin, and Priscilla Meyer, *Nabokov's World, Vol. 1: The Shape of Nabokov's World* (New York: Palgrave, 2002) and *Nabokov's World, Vol. 2: Reading Nabokov* (New York: Palgrave, 2002); Ellen Pifer, ed., *Vladimir Nabokov's Lolita: A Casebook* (New York: Oxford University Press, 2003) (Especially useful in these books are the essays by Rachel Bowlby, John Haegert, Thomas R. Frosch, and Ellen Pifer); Michael Wood, *The Magician's Doubts: Nabokov and the Risks of Fiction* (Princeton: Princeton University Press, 1994).

Articles: Alfred Appel, Jr., "*Lolita:* The Springboard of Parody," *Wisconsin Studies in Contemporary Literature* 8.2: A Special Number Devoted to Vladimir Nabokov (Spring 1967): 204–41; Alfred Appel, Jr., "The Road to *Lolita,* or the Americanization of an Emigre," *JML* 4.1 (September 1974): 3–31; Brian Boyd, "'Even Homais Nods': Nabokov's Fallibility, or, How to Revise *Lolita,*" *Nabokov Studies* 4 (1995): 1–28; Dana Brand, "The Interaction of Aestheticism and American Consumer Culture in Nabokov's *Lolita,*" *Modern Language Studies* 17.2 (Spring 1987): 14–21; Maurice Couturier, "Narcissism and Demand in *Lolita,*" *Nabokov Studies* 9 (2005): 13–34; Paul Giles, "*Lolita,* Pornography, and the Perversions of American Studies," *Journal of American Studies* 34.11 (April 2000): 41–66; Eric Goldman, "'Knowing' Lolita: Sexual Deviance and Normality in Nabokov's *Lolita,*" *Nabokov Studies* 8 (2004): 23–39; Arthur R. Moore, "How Unreliable is Humbert in *Lolita*?" *JML* 25.1 (Autumn 2001): 71–80; Lance Olsen, "A Janus-Faced Text: Realism, Fantasy, and Nabokov's *Lolita,*" *MFS* 32.1 (Spring 1986): 115–25; James Phelan, "Estranging Unreliability, Bonding Unreliability, and the Ethics of *Lolita,*" *Narrative* 15.2 (May 2007): 3–23; Eric Rothstein, "*Lolita:* Nymphet at Normal School," *Contemporary Literature* 41.1 (Spring 2000): 22–55; Alan Singer, "Reasonable Imaginings: Learning from Imagination," *Symploke* 16.1–2 (2008): 227–40; J. B. Sisson, "Nabokov's Cosmic Synchronization and 'Something Else,'" *Nabokov Studies* 1 (1994): 113–34; Nomi Tamir-Ghez, "The Art of Persuasion in Nabokov's *Lolita,*" *Poetics Today* 1.1–2 (1979): 73–90; Frederick S. Whiting, "'The Strange Particularity of the Lover's Preference': Pedophilia, Pornography, and the Anatomy of Monstrosity in *Lolita,*" *American Literature* 70.4 (December 1998): 833–62; Michael Wood, "*Lolita* Revisited," *New England Review* 17.33 (Summer 1995): 15–43. I agree generally with Wood's controversial view that "Humbert's showy self-consciousness, I think, adds up to something less than skepticism: he really is saying what he pretends he is only pretending to say" (28).

3. See my *Lionel Trilling: The Work of Liberation* (Madison: University of Wisconsin Press, 1988).

4. Vladimir Nabokov, *Lectures on Don Quixote,* ed. Fredson Bowers; foreword by Guy Davenport (New York: Harcourt, Brace, Jovanovich, 1983), p. 1: "A masterpiece of fiction is an original world and as such is not likely to fit the world of the reader." Vladimir Nabokov, *Lectures on Literature,* ed. Fredson Bowers; introduction by John Updike (New York: Harcourt, Brace, Jovanovich, 1980), p.1: "We should always remember that the work of art is invariably the creation of

a new world, so that the first thing we should do is to study that new world as closely as possible, approaching it as something brand new, having no obvious connection with the worlds we already know." The other texts by Nabokov cited in this essay are *Speak, Memory: An Autobiography Revisited* (New York: Vintage, 1967); and *Strong Opinions* (New York: Vintage, 1990).

5. See, for just two examples, Philippe Lacoue-Labarth and Jean-Luc Nancy, *The Literary Absolute: The Theory of Literature in German Romanticism* (Binghamton: SUNY Press, 1988); and Pierre Bourdieu, *The Rule of Art: Genesis and Structure of the Literary Field* (Stanford: Stanford University Press, 1996).

6. For a discussion of this topic, see my *The Romance of Interpretation: Visionary Criticism from Pater to De Man* (New York: Columbia University Press, 1985).

7. See Christopher Norris, *Spinoza and the Origins of Modern Critical Theory* (Oxford: Blackwell, 1991).

8. Michael L. Morgan, ed., *The Essential Spinoza: Ethics and Related Writings,* trans. Samuel Shirley (Indianapolis/Cambridge: Hackett, 2006). All citations to this edition will be given hereafter in my text. For a clarifying if at points problematic essay on intuition in Spinoza, see Syliane Malinowski-Charles, "The Circle of Adequate Knowledge," *Oxford Studies in Early Modern Philosophy,* Vol. 1, ed. Daniel Garber and Steven Nadler (New York: Oxford University Press, 2004), pp. 139–63. This commentator argues that traditional views of intuition in Spinoza, especially in Anglo-American and French contexts, have only recently been properly corrected. Malinowski-Charles claims that intuition, the third kind of knowledge like God's, is based in reason, and the second kind, even as it and reason are separated from the first kind, knowledge of the senses is determined by the imagination. I agree that intuition is knowledge of the essence of a particular thing, but it is also knowledge of the whole in the light of eternity, that is, of the processes of being in all their phases in an instant of time: God's knowledge. This intellectual intuition is like neither the sensuous imagination nor the calculating reason, but instead it is indeed a distinctly third kind of knowledge, that of being in all its phases, like the summary-histories of sub-atomic particulars that the mathematical formulas of quantum physics make possible to envision. This is why Spinoza sometimes speaks of intuition as being knowledge of the mind of God. Given that this mind is infinite, for a finite being to have such potent knowledge, even for an instant, is surely a risky proposition, as well as what Spinoza stressed, that accession to power that a divine joy.

9. See explained Nabokov's similar idea, "the springboard of parody," in the article by that title by Appel listed in note 2. For my discussion of Nietzsche on this topic, see my *The Art of Reading as a Way of Life: On Nietzsche's Truth* (Evanston: Northwestern University Press, 2009).

10. See my *The Art of Reading as a Way of Life: On Nietzsche's Truth.*

11. For a discussion of this topic, see my *Visions of Global America and the*

Future of Critical Reading (Columbus: The Ohio State University Press, 2009).

12. For a detailed discussion of this topic, see my *Lionel Trilling: The Work of Liberation* cited previously.

Chapter 4

1. William S. Burroughs, *Naked Lunch: 50th Anniversary Edition, The Restored Text,* ed. James Grauerholz and Barry Miles (New York: Grove Press, 2009). The other Burroughs texts used for this essay are as follows: *The Adding Machine: Selected Essays* (New York: Arcade, 1993); *Early Routines* (Santa Barbara, CA: Cadmus Editions, 1981); *Everything Lost: The Latin American Notebook of William S. Burroughs,* ed. Oliver Harris (Columbus: The Ohio State University Press, 2008); *Exterminator* (New York: Penguin Books, 1979); *Interzone,* ed. James Grauerholz (New York: Penguin Books, 1989); *Junky: 50th Anniversary Edition* , ed. Oliver Harris (New York: Penguin Books, 2003); *The Letters of William S. Burroughs, 1945–1959,* ed. Oliver Harris (New York: Penguin Books, 1993); *Queer* (New York: Penguin Books, 1987); *The Yage Letters Redux,* ed. Oliver Harris (San Francisco: City Lights Books, 2006). The Yage letters are the letters between Burroughs and Ginsberg on the topic of the former's quest for "the ultimate fix" via heroin.

2. The books that have been most helpful are Phil Baker, *William S. Burroughs:* Critical Lives (London: Reaktion Books, 2010); Brian T. Edwards, *Morocco Bound: Disorienting America's Maghreb, From Casablanca to The Marrakech Express* (Durham and London: Duke University Press, 2005); Dennis A. Foster: *Sublime Enjoyment: On the Perverse Motive in American Literature* (New York: Cambridge University Press, 1997); Oliver Harris, *William Burroughs and the Secret of Fascination* (Carbondale: Southern Illinois University Press, 2003); Oliver Harris and Ian MacFadden, eds., *Naked Lunch @ 50: Anniversary Essays* (Carbondale: Southern Illinois University Press, 2009); Barry Miles, *William Burroughs: El Hombre Invisible, A Portrait* (New York: Hyperion, 1992); Ted Morgan, *Literary Outlaw: The Life and Times of William S. Burroughs* (New York: Avon Books, 1990); Timothy S. Murphy, *Wising Up the Marks: The Amodern William Burroughs* (Berkeley: University of California Press, 1997); Davis Schneiderman and Philip Walsh, eds., *Retaking the Universe: William S. Burroughs in the Age of Globalization* (London: Pluto Press, 2004); Rob Wilson, *Beat Attitudes: On the Roads to Beatitude for Post-Beat Writers, Dharma Bums, and Cultural-Political Activists* (San Francisco: New Pacific Press, 2010).

3. See, among other essays, Douglas G. Baldwin, "'Word Begets Image and Image Is Virus': Undermining Language and Film in the Works of William S. Burroughs," *College Literature* 27.1 (Winter 2000): 63–83; Kathryn Hume, "William Burroughs's Phantasmic Geography," *Contemporary Literature* 40.1 (Spring

1999): 111–35; Allan Johnston, "Consumption, Addiction, Vision, Energy: Political Economies and Utopian Visions in the Writings of the Beat Generation," *College Literature* 32.2 (Spring 2005): 103–26; Robin Lydenberg, "Notes from the Orifice: Language and the Body in William Burroughs," *Contemporary Literature* 26.1 (Spring 1985): 55–73; Fiona Paton, "Monstrous Rhetoric: *Naked Lunch*, National Security, and the Gothic Fifties," *Texas Studies in Literature and Language* 52.1 (Spring 2010): 48–69; Wayne Pounds, "The Postmodern Anus: Parody and Utopia in Two Recent Novels by William S. Burroughs," *Poetics Today* 8.3–4 (1987): 611–29; Frederick S. Whiting, "Monstrosity on Trial: The Case of *Naked Lunch*," *Twentieth Century Literature* 52.2 (Summer 2006): 145–74.

4. For Spinoza, see Rebecca Goldstein, *Betraying Spinoza: The Renegade Jew Who Gave Us Modernity* (New York: Schocken, 2006); John Leslie, *Infinite Minds: A Philosophical Cosmology* (New York: Oxford, 2003); Michael L. Morgan, ed., *The Essential Spinoza: Ethics and Related Writings,* trans. Samuel Shirley (Indianapolis/Cambridge: Hackett Publishing Co., 2006). Leslie's vision is remarkably akin to Gilles Deleuze's in his works on Spinoza, but simply clearer for an English-speaking audience. My assumption here is that Burroughs, despite sounding like a latter-day Gnostic, especially in his later work, is an immanentist and that his God is split but one, and one with Nature, rather than two, an evil and incompetent Demiurge and an Alien God beyond existence whose Son must somehow mediate between him and us. In short, like Spinoza, Burroughs's God is the name for that highest state of energy that one may knowingly enjoy without dying or going mad for good. The coincidence via intuition between the finite human mind and the infinite mind of God is thus ever a risky but seductively dangerous proposition: knowledge thus is power and *jouissance.*

Works Cited

Adorno, Theodor. *Philosophy of Modern Music.* Trans. Anne G. Mitchell and Wesley V. Blomster. New York and London: Continuum, 2004.

Alexandrov, Vladimir E. *Nabokov's Otherworld.* Princeton: Princeton University Press, 1991.

Appel, Alfred, Jr. "*Lolita:* The Springboard of Parody." *Wisconsin Studies in Contemporary Literature* 8.2: A Special Number Devoted to Vladimir Nabokov (Spring 1967): 204–41.

———. "The Road to *Lolita,* or the Americanization of an Émigré." *Journal of Modern Literature* 4.1 (September 1974): 3–31.

Baker, Phil. *William S. Burroughs: Critical Lives.* London: Reaktion Books, 2010.

Baldwin, Douglas G. "'Word Begets Image and Image Is Virus': Undermining Language and Film in the Works of William S. Burroughs." *College Literature* 27.1 (Winter 2000): 63–83.

Beddow, Michael. *Mann:* Doctor Faustus. Landmarks of World Literature Series. Cambridge: Cambridge University Press, 1994.

Blackmur, R. P. *Eleven Essays in the European Novel.* New York: Harcourt, Brace & World, Inc., 1964.

Bloom, Harold. "Clinamen, or Poetic Misprision." *New Literary History* 3.2: On Interpretation: I (Winter 1972): 373–91.

Bourdieu, Pierre. *The Rule of Art: Genesis and Structure of the Literary Field.* Stanford: Stanford University Press, 1996.

Bove, Paul. "Misprisions of Utopia: Messianism, Modernism, and Allegory," In *A Preface to Henry Adams.* Cambridge: Harvard University Press.

Boyd, Brian. "'Even Homais Nods': Nabokov's Fallibility, or, How to Revise *Lolita.*" *Nabokov Studies* 4 (1995): 1–28.

———. *Vladimir Nabokov: The American Years.* New York: Vintage, 1991.

———. *Vladimir Nabokov: The Russian Years.* Princeton: Princeton University Press, 1990.

Brand, Dana. "The Interaction of Aestheticism and American Consumer Culture in Nabokov's *Lolita.*" *Modern Language Studies* 17.2 (Spring 1987): 14–21.

Bromwich, David. "Reflections on the Word Genius." *New Literary History* 17.1: Philosophy of Science and Literary Theory (Autumn 1985): 141–64.

Burkholder, J. Peter et al., eds. *A History of Western Music.* 8th ed. New York: W. W. Norton, Inc., 2010.

Burroughs, William S. *The Adding Machine: Selected Essays.* New York: Arcade, 1993.

———. *Early Routines.* Santa Barbara, CA: Cadmus Editions, 1981.

———. *Everything Lost: The Latin American Notebook of William S. Burroughs.* Ed. Oliver Harris. Columbus: The Ohio State University Press, 2008.

———. *Exterminator.* New York: Penguin Books, 1979.

———. *Interzone.* Ed. James Grauerholz. New York: Penguin Books, 1989.

———. *Junky: 50th Anniversary Edition.* Ed. Oliver Harris. New York: Penguin Books, 2003.

———. *The Letters of William S. Burroughs, 1945–1959.* Ed. Oliver Harris. New York: Penguin Books, 1993.

———. *Naked Lunch: 50th Anniversary Edition, The Restored Text.* Ed. James Grauerholz and Barry Miles. New York: Grove Press, 2009.

———. *Queer.* New York: Penguin Books, 1987.

———. *The Yage Letters Redux.* Ed. Oliver Harris. San Francisco: City Lights Books, 2006.

Byrne, Laura. "The Geometrical Method in Spinoza's *Ethics.*" *Poetics Today* 28.3 (Fall 2007): 441–74.

Christensen, Jerome C. "The Genius in the *Biographia Literaria.*" *Studies in Romanticism* 17.2 (Spring 1978): 215–31.

Connolly, Julian W., ed. *The Cambridge Companion to Nabokov.* New York: Cambridge University Press, 2005.

———. *A Reader's Guide to* Lolita. Boston: Academic Studies Press, 2009.

Copleston, F. C. "Spinoza and Pantheism." *Philosophy* 21.78 (April 1946): 42–56.

Couturier, Maurice. "Narcissism and Demand in *Lolita.*" *Nabokov Studies* 9 (2005): 13–34.

Deleuze, Gilles. *Expressionism in Philosophy: Spinoza.* Trans. Martin Joughlin. New York: Zone Books, 1992.

Della Rocca, Michael. "Spinoza and the Metaphysics of Scepticism." *Mind* 116.464 (October 2007): 851–74.

Derrida, Jacques. *Geneses, Genealogies, Genres, and Genius: The Secrets of the Archive.* Trans. Beverley Bie Brahic. New York: Columbia University Press, 2006.

Drassinower, Abraham. *Freud's Theory of Culture: Eros, Loss, and Politics.* Lanham and New York: Rowan & Littlefield Publishers, Inc., 2003.

Edwards, Brian T. *Morocco Bound: Disorienting America's Maghreb, From Casablanca to The Marrakech Express.* New Americanists Series. Durham and London: Duke University Press, 2005.

Fetzer, John F. *Changing Perceptions of Thomas Mann's* Doctor Faustus: *Criticism 1947–1992.* Columbia, SC: Camden House, 1996.

Foster, Dennis A. *Sublime Enjoyment: On the Perverse Motive in American Literature.* New York: Cambridge University Press, 1997.

Freud, Sigmund. *Beyond the Pleasure Principle and Other Writings.* Trans. John Reddick. Introduction by Mark Edumnson. New York: Penguin Books, 2003.

Giles, Paul. "*Lolita,* Pornography, and the Perversions of American Studies." *Journal of American Studies* 34.1 (April 2000): 41–66.

Goldman, Eric. "'Knowing' Lolita: Sexual Deviance and Normality in Nabokov's *Lolita.*" *Nabokov Studies* 8 (2004): 23–39.

Goldstein, Rebecca. *Betraying Spinoza: The Renegade Jew Who Gave Us Modernity.* New York: Schocken, 2006.

Grayson, Jane, Arnold McMillin, and Priscilla Meyer. *Nabokov's World, Vol. 1: The Shape of Nabokov's World.* New York: Palgrave, 2002.

———. *Nabokov's World, Vol. 2: Reading Nabokov.* New York: Palgrave, 2002.

Harris, Oliver. *William Burroughs and the Secret of Fascination.* Carbondale: Southern Illinois University Press, 2003.

——— and Ian McFadden, eds. *Naked Lunch @ 50: Anniversary Essays.* Carbondale: Southern Illinois University Press, 2009.

Heilbut, Anthony. *Thomas Mann: Eros and Literature.* Berkeley and Los Angeles: University of California Press, 1995.

Hume, Kathryn. "William Burroughs's Phantasmic Geography." *Contemporary Literature* 40.1 (Spring 1999): 111–35.

Jameson, Fredric. "Allegory and History: Rereading *Doctor Faustus.*" *The Modernist Papers.* London: Verso, 2007. 91–123.

Johnston, Allan. "Consumption, Addiction, Vision, Energy: Political Economies and Utopian Visions in the Writings of the Beat Generation." *College Literature* 32.2 (Spring 2005).

Joyce, James. *Dubliners: Critical Edition.* Ed. Margot Norris. New York: W. W. Norton, 2006. 311–12.

Kaufmann, Fritz. "Spinoza's System as Theory of Expression." *Philosophy and Phenomenological Research* 1.1 (September 1940): 83–97.

Kurzke, Hermann. *Thomas Mann: Life as a Work of Art.* Trans. Leslie Wilson. Princeton and Oxford: Princeton University Press, 2002.

Lacoue-Labarthe, Phillipe and Jean-Luc Nancy. *The Literary Absolute: The Theory of Literature in German Romanticism.* Trans. Philip Barnard and Cheryl Lester. Albany: SUNY Press, 1988.

Lee, Frances. *Overturning* Doctor Faustus: *Rereading Thomas Mann's Novel in*

Light of Observations of a Non-Political Man. Columbia, SC: Camden House, 2007.

Leslie, John. *Infinite Minds: A Philosophical Cosmology.* New York: Oxford University Press, 2003.

Lewis, C. S. "Genius and Genius." *The Review of English Studies* 12.46 (April 1936): 189–94.

Lydenberg, Robin. "Notes from the Orifice: Language and the Body in William Burroughs." *Contemporary Literature* 26.1 (Spring 1985): 55–73.

Malinowski-Charles, Syliane. "The Circle of Adequate Knowledge." *Oxford Studies in Early Modern Philosophy.* Vol. 1. Ed. Daniel Garber and Steven Nadler. New York: Oxford University Press, 2004. 139–63.

McFarland, Thomas. *Coleridge and the Pantheist Tradition.* Oxford: Oxford University Press at the Clarendon Press, 1969.

———. *Originality and Imagination.* Baltimore and London: The Johns Hopkins University Press, 1985.

Mann, Thomas. *Death in Venice.* Trans. Michael Henry Heim. Introduction by Michael Cunningham. New York: HarperCollins, 2004.

———. *Diaries, 1918–1939.* Selection and Foreword by Hermann Kesten. Trans. Richard and Clara Winston. London: Robin Clark, 1984.

———. *Doctor Faustus: The Life of the German Composer Adrian Leverkühn as Told by a Friend.* Trans. John E. Woods. New York: Vintage, 1997.

———. *Doctor Faustus.* Trans. H. T. Lowe-Porter. New York: The Modern Library, 1948.

———. *Doktor Faustus.* Frankfurt am Main, Germany: S. Fischer Verlag, 2007.

———. "Freud and the Future." *Essays of Three Decades.* Trans. H. T. Lowe-Porter. New York: Knopf, 1947. 411–28.

———. *Reflections of a Non-Political Man.* Trans. Walter D. Norris. New York: Fredrick Ungar, 1983.

———. *Stories of Three Decades.* Trans. H. T. Lowe-Porter. New York: Knopf, 1936.

———. *The Story of a Novel: The Genesis of Doctor Faustus.* Trans. Richard and Clara Winston. New York: Knopf, 1961.

Miles, Barry. *William Burroughs: El Hombre Invisible, A Portrait.* New York: Hyperion, 1992.

Miller, Perry. "Emersonian Genius and the American Democracy." *The New England Quarterly* 26.1 (March 1953): 27–44.

Moore, Arthur R. "How Unreliable Is Humbert in *Lolita?*" *Journal of Modern Literature* 25.1 (Autumn 2001): 71–80.

Morgan, Michael, ed. *The Essential Spinoza: Ethics and Related Writings.* Trans. Samuel Shirley. Indianapolis and London: Hackett, 2006.

Morgan, Ted. *Literary Outlaw: The Life and Times of William S. Burroughs.* New York: Avon Books, 1990.

Morrison, James C. "Why Spinoza Had No Aesthetics." *The Journal of Aesthetics and Art Criticism* 47.4 (Autumn 1989): 359–65.

Murphy, Timothy S. *Wising Up the Marks: The Amodern William Burroughs.* Berkeley: University of California Press, 1997.

Murray, Penelope, ed. *Genius: The History of an Idea.* Oxford: Blackwell, 1989.

Nabokov, Vladimir. *The Annotated Lolita,* revised and updated. Ed. Alfred Appel, Jr. New York: Vintage, 1991.

———. *Lectures on Don Quixote.* Ed. Fredson Bowers. Foreword by Guy Davenport. New York: Harcourt, Brace, Jovanovich, 1983.

———. *Lectures on Literature.* Ed. Fredson Bowers. Introduction by John Updike. New York: Harcourt, Brace, Jovanovich, 1980.

———. *Speak, Memory: An Autobiography Revisited.* New York: Vintage, 1967.

———. *Strong Opinions.* New York: Vintage, 1990.

Nadler, Steven. "Spinoza and Consciousness." *Mind* 117.467 (July 2008): 575–601.

———. *Spinoza's Ethics: An Introduction.* New York: Cambridge University Press, 2006.

Norris, Christopher. *Spinoza and the Origins of Modern Critical Theory.* Oxford: Blackwell, 1991.

Nussbaum, Martha. "The Ascent of Love: Plato, Spinoza, Proust." *New Literary History* 25.4: 25th Anniversary Issue (Part 2) (Autumn 1994): 925–49.

O'Hara, Daniel. *The Art of Reading as a Way of Life: On Nietzsche's Truth.* Evanston: Northwestern University Press, 2009.

———. *Lionel Trilling: The Work of Liberation.* Madison: University of Wisconsin Press, 1988.

———. *Radical Parody: American Culture and Critical Agency after Foucault .* New York: Columbia University Press, 1992.

———. *The Romance of Interpretation: Visionary Criticism from Pater to De Man.* New York: Columbia University Press, 1985.

———. *Visions of Global America and the Future of Critical Reading.* Columbus: The Ohio State University Press, 2009.

Olsen, Lance. "A Janus-Faced Text: Realism, Fantasy, and Nabokov's *Lolita.*" *Modern Fiction Studies* 32.1 (Spring 1986): 115–25.

Parkinson, G. H. R. "Hegel, Pantheism, and Spinoza." *Journal of the History of Ideas* 38.3 (July–September, 1977): 449–59.

Paton, Fiona. "Monstrous Rhetoric: *Naked Lunch,* National Security, and the Gothic Fifties." *Texas Studies in Literature and Language* 52.1 (Spring 2010): 48–69.

Phelan, James. "Estranging Unreliability, Bonding Unreliability, and the Ethics of *Lolita.*" *Narrative* 15.2 (May 2007): 3–23.

Pifer, Ellen, ed. *Vladimir Nabokov's* Lolita: *A Casebook.* New York: Oxford University Press, 2003.

Pounds, Wayne. "The Postmodern Anus: Parody and Utopia in Two Recent Novels by William S. Burroughs." *Poetics Today* 8.3/4 (1987): 611–29.

Rothstein, Eric. "*Lolita:* Nymphet at Normal School." *Contemporary Literature* 41.1 (Spring 2000): 22–55.

Said, Edward W. *Musical Elaborations.* New York: Columbia University Press, 1991.

Schneiderman, Davis and Philip Walsh, eds. *Retaking the Universe: William S. Burroughs in the Age of Globalization.* London: Pluto Press, 2004.

Schoenberg, Arthur. *Theory of Harmony.* Trans. Roy E. Carter. Berkeley and Los Angeles: University of California Press, 1983.

Singer, Alan. "Reasonable Imaginings: Learning from Imagination." *Symploke* 16.1–2 (2008): 227–40.

Sisson, J. B. "Nabokov's Cosmic Synchronization and 'Something Else.'" *Nabokov Studies* 1 (1994): 113–34.

Spinoza, Benedictus de. *The Essential Spinoza: Ethics and Related Writings.* Ed. Michael L. Morgan. Trans. Samuel Shirley. Indianapolis and Cambridge: Hackett, 2006.

Stadler, Gustavus. *Troubling Minds: The Cultural Politics of Genius in the United States, 1840–1890.* Minneapolis: University of Minnesota Press, 2006.

Tamir-Ghez, Nomi. "The Art of Persuasion in Nabokov's *Lolita.*" *Poetics Today* 1.1–2 (1979): 73–90.

Trilling, Lionel. *The Moral Obligation to Be Intelligent.* Ed. with an Introduction by Leon Wieseltier. New York: Farrar, Strauss and Giroux, 2000.

———. *Prefaces to the Experience of Literature.* New York: Harvest Books, 1981.

Virtanen, Ralph. "On the Dichotomy between Genius and Talent." *Comparative Literature Studies* 18.1 (March 1981): 69–90.

Walker, Ralph C. "Spinoza and the Coherence Theory of Truth." *Mind New Series* 94.373 (January 1985): 1–18.

Weiss, Piero and Richard Taruskin. *Music in the Western World: A History in Documents.* 2nd ed. Belmont, CA: Schirmer Cengage Learning, 2008.

Whiting, Frederick S. "Monstrosity on Trial: The Case of *Naked Lunch.*" *Twentieth Century Literature* 52.2 (Summer 2006): 145–74.

———. "'The Strange Particularity of the Lover's Preference': Pedophilia, Pornography, and the Anatomy of Monstrosity in *Lolita.*" *American Literature* 70.4 (December 1998): 833–62.

Wilson, Rob. *Beat Attitudes: On the Roads to Beatitude for Post-Beat Writers, Dharma Bums, and Cultural-Political Activists.* San Francisco: New Pacific Press, 2010.

Wolstein, Benjamin. "The Romantic Spinoza in America." *Journal of the History of Ideas* 14.3 (June 1953): 439–50.

Wood, Michael. "*Lolita* Revisited." *New England Review* 17.3 (Summer 1995): 15–43.

———. *The Magician's Doubts: Nabokov and the Risks of Fiction.* Princeton: Princeton University Press, 1994.

Index